For more tools and training, visit us on cirruspublishing.net or use the QR code below to reach our site.

ILLUMINATING BUSINESS DECISIONS:

A Practical Guide

Chance Mixon

Copyright © 2024 Cirrus Publishing

All rights reserved. No portion of this book may be reproduced mechanically, electronically, or by any other means, including photocopying, without permission of the publisher or author except in the case of brief quotations embodied in critical articles and reviews. It is illegal to copy this book, post it to a website, or distribute it by any other means without permission from the publisher or author.

CONTENTS

Understanding Business Decision-Making 9
    The Foundation of Strategic Planning 9
    Embracing Data-Driven Decisions 12
    Integrating Strategy and Analytics in Decision-Making 14
    References 15

Frameworks for Effective Decision Evaluation 16
    Harnessing SWOT for Strategic Insights 16
    The Power of Cost-Benefit Analysis in Decision-Making 19
    Leveraging Scenario Planning for Future Preparedness 21
    Decision Trees: Visualizing Choices and Outcomes 23
    Strategic Tools for Enhanced Decision-Making 26
    References 27

Data-Driven Decision-Making Strategies 30
    Leveraging Statistical Models for Predictive Analytics 30
    Interpreting Data Trends for Strategic Insights 33
    Enhancing Decision Clarity with Data Visualization 35
    Implementing Machine Learning for Predictive Modeling 37
    References 41

Risk Mitigation and Opportunity Seizure 44
    Introducing Risk Mitigation Strategies 44
    Identifying Opportunities Through Market Analysis 46
    Seizing Competitive Advantages 50
    Adapting to Market Uncertainties with Agility 52
    Enhancing Decision-Making Processes 55
    References 57

Strategic Decision-Making in Real-World Scenarios ... 59
- Applying Strategic Decision-Making Through Case Studies ... 60
- Strategic Decision-Making Across Various Business Contexts ... 62
- Learning from Failures to Enhance Future Decisions ... 65
- Distilling Best Practices for Effective Strategic Decision-Making ... 67
- Essential Takeaways for Mastering Strategic Decision-Making ... 70
- References ... 72

Aligning Decisions with Strategic Goals ... 74
- Setting strategic objectives for decision alignment ... 74
- Measuring decision impact on strategic goals ... 77
- Adapting decisions to changing market conditions ... 79
- Ensuring organizational coherence through decisions ... 83
- References ... 87

Leadership's Role in Decision-Making ... 89
- Building Decision-Making Teams for Success ... 89
- Empowering Employees in Decision Processes ... 92
- Cultivating a Culture of Informed Choices ... 94
- Navigating Ethical Considerations in Decision-Making ... 97
- Enhancing Decision-Making Across the Organization ... 99
- References ... 101

Continuous Improvement through Decision Analysis ... 103
- Valuing Post-Decision Analysis ... 103
- Iterative Decision-Making Benefits ... 106
- Feedback Loops for Decision Refinement ... 108
- Advocating for Data-Driven Decision Analysis ... 111
- Harnessing Insights for Superior Decision-Making ... 113
- References ... 114

Decision-Making in Uncertain Environments 116
    Adaptive Decision-Making: Thriving in Volatility 117
    Risk Tolerance in Uncertain Times: Navigating Through Turbulence ... 119
    The Value of Flexibility: Adapting Strategies to Win 122
    Agility and Resilience: Overcoming Unpredictability 125
    Critical Strategies for Decision-Making in Uncertain Environments 128
    References 130
Implementing Decision-Making Best Practices 132
    Building a Decision-Making Toolkit 132
    Cultivating a Decision-Forward Organizational Culture 135
    Strategies for Effective Decision Implementation 137
    References 138

Understanding Business Decision-Making

In the business world, making decisions feels a lot like steering a ship through unknown seas. Every decision can push the company ahead or send it off course. It highlights how tricky and crucial it is to make good calls in this high-stakes environment, where every turn might lead to triumph or trouble.

Thanks to the fast-evolving market and technological leaps, today's businesses are swamped with choices. Decision-makers often find themselves at a fork in the road, weighed down by several factors: economic shifts, changes in what consumers want, the competitive scene, and limits on what resources they have available. The danger of jumping to conclusions without all the facts or making snap judgments is real and can throw even the most hopeful projects off track. Without a solid plan or guide, companies might go with their gut, which, while helpful, can be shaky and generally not enough for the complex business landscape.

The Foundation of Strategic Planning

Strategic planning is like setting your sails when you're about to embark on a voyage across the open sea. Imagine plotting a course for your business's journey, not just bracing for the winds and currents but also ready to zigzag through unexpected storms and opportunities that come your way. This careful, step-by-step approach keeps a business floating and steadily cruising toward its big dreams.

At the heart of strategic planning is the drive to peer into the future, sketch out a path, and make sure today's actions are in lockstep with where you want to end up. It's pretty magical how it transforms foresight into a game plan, letting companies be one step ahead rather than scrambling to catch up. Picture steering your business with a crystal-clear vision of where you aim to be five years later. Strategic planning chops up this dream into smaller, manageable pieces, charting a direction for daily operations and choices. It ensures every bit of effort and resource pours into ventures critical for success, empowering businesses to weave through hurdles with skill and assurance.

Richard F. Vancil and Peter Lorange offered a sharp insight into the world of strategic planning in their Harvard Business Review piece, portraying it as a methodical dance of reevaluating strategy over the years. They talked about identifying both the good and evil, the risks and possibilities, and then crafting various strategic pathways that align with the company's long-term ambitions (Harvard Business Review, 1975). It's a reminder that strategic planning isn't a haphazard affair but a thoughtful, in-depth exploration into a company's path forward, ensuring it stays pertinent and competitive.

Moreover, strategic planning knits together a culture where everybody's rowing in the same direction. A sense of belonging and purpose blooms when the whole crew understands the grand plan and how they fit into it. This camaraderie is vital for keeping conversations flowing and executing strategies smoothly. Teams in their bubbles might miss the magic when diverse minds and talents target a unified objective.

Digging into the bit about making wise choices, strategic planning is more than picking a route; it's about thoroughly vetting each possibility, weighing its practicality, impact, and how well it vibes with the company's core beliefs and targets. This is where strategic planning makes its mark - offering a solid framework that weighs ambition against reality and innovation against lasting value.

Yet, for strategic planning to take root within a company's culture, it calls for ongoing tweaking and enhancement. The business world is constantly in flux, pushed and pulled by new tech, market trends, competition, and consumer tastes. Therefore, strategic plans can't just sit pretty on a shelf; they need to be dynamic blueprints that are revisited and refreshed to stay relevant and ambitious. Adopting this flexible stance ensures a business can adjust its game plan effectively when faced with new challenges or opportunities, keeping it at the forefront of its field.

Peeling back another layer of strategic planning involves checking out specific steps, particularly when thinking about the challenges and chances that lie ahead:

Start by conducting a deep dive into market analysis to spot emerging trends, threats, and overlooked opportunities. This should cover not only the immediate competition but also wider industry shifts and breakthroughs.

Running a SWOT analysis (Strengths, Weaknesses, Opportunities, Threats) offers a bird' s-eye view of your company's current situation and potential future, highlighting areas of advantage and areas needing improvement.

Venturing into scenario planning is also crucial. By imagining future market conditions and assessing how your company would hold up under each, you can pinpoint strategies that stand firm no matter what tomorrow brings.

Remember, strategic planning doesn't fall solely on the shoulders of top brass. It thrives on contributions from every corner of the organization. Opening the floor to input from different departments injects a wealth of perspectives into the mix, building a sense of unity and shared commitment toward the company's goals.

Embracing Data-Driven Decisions

In the hustle and bustle of today's business world, having data-driven strategies is like holding a compass that steers companies through the challenging seas of competition and innovation. The era when decisions were solely made from gut feelings or instinct has faded away. Now, it's the era of digits and stats. Picture yourself navigating a ship across the vast ocean without a compass; you'd be at a loss, right? But with one, your direction is much more precise. Similarly, data gives businesses a well-defined route based on facts and patterns.

You might ask, why is there a significant move towards data? It turns out that using analytics and concrete data allows businesses to make choices grounded in solid evidence, leaving less room for mere guesses. This approach helps cut down biases, which can easily trip up decision-making by depending on tangible insights for guidance. It's comparable to following a trail in the forest because you've seen signs that it leads to where you want to go rather than just feeling it might take you there.

Moreover, embracing a data-centric mindset comes with its perks. It significantly boosts operational efficiency, making everything work smoother, faster, and with fewer resources, yet achieving better results. Imagine stumbling upon a shortcut that saves time and avoids hazards. On top of that, it fuels innovation by uncovering trends and connections that aren't immediately obvious at first glance. It's similar to cooking up a brand-new dish by figuring out which ingredients blend ideally based on past trials.

However, shifting gears towards data isn't a walk in the park. A significant bump on this road is getting everyone onboard with understanding the importance of data and mastering its use. Here are some actionable steps to smooth out this challenge:

- Start with training sessions to raise data literacy throughout the organization. This ensures everybody is on the same page about data.

- Introduce easy-to-use tools that demystify data analysis for the non-tech savvy. Not all are data wizards, but anyone can uncover valuable insights from data with straightforward tools.

- Build a culture that values and rewards data-driven decisions. This will motivate the team to rely more on data rather than just going with their gut.

While the power of data in refining business choices is undeniable, it's also crucial to remember that data isn't perfect. Issues like data quality, accurate interpretation, and the risk of relying on outdated information can skew decisions. Hence, a balanced strategy is critical, where data lays the groundwork for choices supported by contextual insights and critical thinking. Think of it as using a map; it points out the roads, but navigating through traffic is still up to you.

At its core, turning a business into one guided by data resembles tuning an instrument. Done right, it creates harmony among different aspects of the company, leading to improved efficiency, innovation, and, in the long run, sustainable growth. Yet, it demands meticulous care, ongoing education, and the ability to adapt, ensuring the business remains aligned with changing market trends.

Integrating Strategy and Analytics in Decision-Making

Throughout this chapter, we've explored the art of strategic planning and the power of making well-informed decisions in the fast-paced world of business. We liken strategic planning to embarking on a voyage into unknown waters, equipped with the resilience and agility to face any challenges head-on. This journey highlighted the significance of plotting a path toward our aspirations and ensuring every action aligns with our deepest values and long-term goals.

The insights shared here are especially pertinent for those in the business field. We're witnessing a shift toward relying more heavily on data when making decisions. It's a new chapter where gut feelings are backed up by hard facts, enabling sharper navigation through the competitive twists and turns of the business environment.

Yet embracing data comes with its own set of hurdles. It's crucial for everyone in an organization to grasp and value what data can offer. The challenge lies in marrying innovation with tradition, ambition with pragmatism, and striking a balance that ensures growth and success are sustainable over time.

References

Ansoff, H. I. (1975). *Strategic planning in diversified companies.* Harvard Business Review, 3751. https://hbr.org/1975/01/strategic-planning-in-diversified-companiesHBS Online. (2019). *The Advantages of Data-Driven Decision-Making. Business Insights Blog.* Retrieved from https://online.hbs.edu/blog/post/data-driven-decision-makingHBS Online. (2020). *Why is strategic planning important? Business Insights Blog.* Retrieved from https://online.hbs.edu/blog/post/why-is-strategic-planning-importantHarvard Online. (2022). *How data science can benefit your business decisions. Blog.* Retrieved from https://www.harvardonline.harvard.edu/blog/how-data-science-can-benefit-your-business-decisionsIMD Business School. (2023). *What is Strategic Planning, & Why is it Important?* [Website]. https://www.imd.org/reflections/what-is-strategic-planning-why-is-it-important/University of Pennsylvania. (n.d.). *5 key reasons data analytics is essential in business.* Retrieved from https://lpsonline.sas.upenn.edu/features/5-key-reasons-why-data-analytics-important-business

Frameworks for Effective Decision Evaluation

In business, making choices is like trying to find your way in a constantly shifting scene. Each decision comes with its possible gains and losses, requiring a thoughtful review of all options to decide on the best path forward. This changing environment is a challenge for even the most experienced professionals, who must weigh the immediate advantages against what might happen. It's important to emphasize how complicated this process is because it demands an understanding of the current situation and a forecast of what could come next.

A major obstacle in making intelligent decisions is dealing with the uncertainty that seems part of many business situations. Every choice has some risk, like investing in technology that may soon be obsolete or stepping into a market that turns out to be more competitive than you thought. Figuring out these risks while spotting possible opportunities is crucial but can feel overwhelming. Without a systematic way of making these choices, companies might rely on partial information or, even worse, go with their gut feeling. This approach can lead to decisions that seem right in the short run but don't fit the company's long-term plans or goals.

Harnessing SWOT for Strategic Insights

Grasping the significance of SWOT analysis in making strategic decisions is essential in today's fast-paced business world. At its heart, SWOT analysis is a tool that helps companies examine their internal and external environments by pointing out strengths, weaknesses, opportunities, and threats. This approach provides a well-rounded perspective, encouraging companies to celebrate their successes and address their shortcomings and the dangers they may encounter.

For any company, recognizing its strengths involves appreciating those unique qualities that set it apart from competitors, like a strong brand presence, loyal customers, or cutting-edge products and services. Highlighting these positive aspects boosts morale and gives a company leverage in its industry. Yet, that's only part of the story. Companies must also bravely face their weaknesses—those internal factors that could impede progress. Acknowledging these issues is the first step towards improvement, whether it's insufficient funds, outdated technology, or gaps in employee skills. It's crucial to understand that all companies have flaws; what matters is how they proactively identify and tackle them.

Looking beyond the company walls, opportunities are abundant and can lead to significant growth and achievement if utilized correctly. These changes might come from new market trends, technological breakthroughs, or shifts in consumer behavior. However, while pursuing these opportunities, companies must be ready for threats like economic downturns, increasing competition, or regulation changes. A readiness plan and strategies to mitigate these risks can be game-changers.

Now, harmonizing what a company does best with external chances while keeping an eye on threats requires a deliberate strategy. This is where following specific steps becomes helpful. Start by gathering detailed information about your company and the market, including data from market studies, financial reports, and analyses of competitors. Then, involve team members from various departments in the SWOT analysis to provide different perspectives, possibly shedding light on aspects you still need to consider. After that, rank the identified factors based on how they might affect your business objectives. Finally, devise a strategic action plan targeting these key areas to use strengths, improve weak points, capture opportunities, and guard against threats.

Furthermore, SWOT analysis can highlight where to channel resources and efforts for improvement. This might mean investing in new technology to stay ahead or providing staff training to boost their skills. By identifying these needs, businesses can take focused actions likely to pay off significantly over time.

Importantly, SWOT analysis guides leaders in prioritizing initiatives based on strategic insights. When faced with choices, this framework helps evaluate different paths about the business's strategic position and the external environment. This leads to more thoughtful, informed decisions that consider the long-term implications for the company's direction.

SWOT analysis's flexibility makes it an invaluable resource for addressing various business challenges, whether considering a new venture, launching a product, or developing corporate strategies. It offers clarity and direction, aiding companies in moving towards survival and flourishing in a complex business arena (SWOT Analysis: How to Strengthen Your Business Plan, n.d.).

At its essence, the strength of SWOT analysis is its straightforward yet profound nature. It compels organizations to closely examine their strengths and limitations and the broader market landscape. When executed well, it transcends being a mere academic task; it becomes a strategic beacon that directs companies toward lasting achievements. What makes SWOT particularly powerful is its promotion of honesty and transparency in assessing where a business stands today and where it could be tomorrow. Encouraging a strategic mindset, SWOT analysis propels continuous advancement and innovation. In an ever-changing world, thoroughly understanding your company's internal dynamics and the external forces at play is priceless.

The Power of Cost-Benefit Analysis in Decision-Making

Understanding the role of Cost-Benefit Analysis (CBA) in making choices is like having a navigation tool when you're making big decisions in an organization. Think of CBA as a method that helps put numbers to the pros and cons, shining a light on the best path forward through unclear situations. It turns the often vague idea of what we might gain or lose into something concrete, helping us see what's at stake with each decision.

When applying CBA, it's crucial to thoroughly identify all possible costs—not just the obvious ones, like expenses related to carrying out a project, but also the not-so-obvious ones, like opportunities we miss out on by choosing one option over another. This detailed listing ensures that every financial aspect is considered, leaving no room for surprises later.

In the same way, being just as rigorous in identifying potential benefits is critical. Benefits are more than just increasing profit; they include less tangible gains such as improved brand reputation and happier employees. Putting a dollar amount on these varied benefits can be challenging, but it's essential for a full picture of what might be gained, requiring a bit of creativity to figure out the value of things that don't traditionally come with price tags.

We can make direct comparisons by converting costs and benefits into monetary terms. Although this process involves some guesswork and forecasting, the goal is to anchor our analysis in as much real data as possible. It's understood that not everything can be precisely quantified, but well-grounded estimates can still offer valuable insight.

This approach does more than just number-crunching; it guides strategic thinking. If the projected benefits exceed the costs, it's a sign that the venture could be worth pursuing. But if it's the other way around, it's a warning that maybe it's time to reconsider. These insights are invaluable for predicting outcomes, guiding where to allocate resources best, and focusing efforts for the greatest return.

It's also important to zoom out and look at the big picture. The outcomes of CBA are influenced by—and can influence—the wider economy, current market conditions, governmental regulations, and societal expectations. This interplay highlights that while CBA is a powerful tool, its effectiveness is boosted when used alongside other analytical methods, reminding us that financial decisions also reflect an organization's values and goals.

Practicing CBA effectively takes skill, vision, and a willingness to acknowledge its limitations, such as possible inaccuracies and the difficulty in valuing intangible benefits. This openness doesn't weaken CBA's usefulness; instead, it positions it as part of a more extensive, evidence-driven strategy in decision-making.

Furthermore, adopting CBA encourages a culture where decisions are made transparently and responsibly. It calls for clear documentation and sharing of the thought process, fostering trust among stakeholders by showing a commitment to careful stewardship of resources aimed at achieving specific objectives.

At its core, Cost-Benefit Analysis transcends being simply a decision-making technique; it embodies a commitment to making choices based on informed reasoning. As we face more intricate challenges today, the foundational elements of CBA—transparency, responsibility, and practical wisdom—serve as beacons guiding us toward decisions that support sustainable success and collective progress.

Leveraging Scenario Planning for Future Preparedness

Scenario planning is a fancy term best suited for the strategy sessions of prominent corporations. Still, it's a beneficial strategy for businesses of all sizes aiming to stay afloat in the unpredictable business environment. Simply put, scenario planning helps organizations prepare for different potential futures, making responding to changes easier and avoiding being caught off guard. This approach doesn't aim to predict the future with pinpoint accuracy—something that's impossible outside science fiction. Instead, it's about getting ready for a variety of possible outcomes.

Understanding the importance of scenario planning sheds light on its ability to help businesses navigate uncertain times. Companies can create flexible strategies by considering how various economic, social, or technological changes could impact their operations. These strategies make them more resilient, enabling them to withstand unforeseen challenges. Given how quickly things can change in the current market, this resilience is becoming a must-have for survival.

Moving onto the practical aspect, implementing scenario planning in your organization involves a few key steps:

- Start by clearly defining your organization's values. Understanding your core mission, values, and unique circumstances acts as your guiding light, helping you make decisions that align with your overarching goals while also considering financial health, employee wellbeing, and fairness.

- Identify which aspects of your business are most vulnerable to change. Concentrating your planning efforts where they're most needed will ensure you're not caught unprepared.

- Create a range of scenarios, from best to worst-case, based on your identified vulnerabilities. This exercise prompts you to think about factors beyond your control and how they could influence your strategic direction.

- Put together a set of strategic responses for each scenario. These should vary from all-encompassing actions that apply to multiple scenarios to specific tactics tailored to particular situations.

Through scenario planning, organizations give themselves a head start in dealing with uncertainties. They're not just reacting to changes but anticipating them and preparing accordingly. The beauty of scenario planning lies in its ability to improve decision-making under uncertainty by evaluating different "what-if" situations. This builds resilience and sharpens the organization's approach to managing risks by testing the strength of its strategies against various potential futures.

Scenario planning's applicability goes beyond the corporate sector, proving useful for nonprofits as well. In a world that doesn't change, nonprofit and for-profit organizations can benefit from a structured method to tackle unpredictability with confidence, maintaining their focus on their missions (Searle et al., 2022).

A real-world application of scenario planning was seen during the COVID-19 pandemic when many organizations faced unprecedented challenges. Using scenario planning, they could envisage multiple outcomes and adapt their strategies in real-time. This proactive approach helped them mitigate the impacts of the pandemic, showing the practical value of being forward-thinking.

Decision Trees: Visualizing Choices and Outcomes

In the complex world of decision-making, whether in business or daily life, having the right tools to chart our course. Decision trees are one such tool worth taking a closer look at. Essentially, decision trees lay out our options visually, helping us understand the potential outcomes of our decisions. This method not only makes the process of making decisions easier but also highlights the possible risks and benefits that come with each option.

When applying decision trees effectively, they provide a structured approach to mapping out decisions, which is particularly useful when facing complex choices with uncertain outcomes. Here's a simple way to use decision trees:

1. Clearly state the problem you're deciding on.
2. List all possible choices and their outcomes, including any risks, benefits, and the chances of each happening.
3. Create the decision tree by putting your first decision at the root and drawing branches for each possible choice and its consequences.

Organizations can use this step-by-step process to assess different decision paths carefully. This helps them understand the expected value of various options, guiding them toward the best decision. It's essential to look beyond short-term results and consider how choices affect the long term.

Decision trees also allow us to evaluate many factors and uncertainties at once. In a fast-moving environment, decisions often require balancing different aspects. To maximize decision trees in these situations, it's helpful to:

- Include stakeholders in the decision-making process for a broader viewpoint.

- Update the decision tree as things change or more information becomes available.
- Use specific software for analyzing decision trees to manage complex scenarios efficiently.

By breaking down complicated decisions into simpler parts, decision trees make the decision-making process more transparent and based on evidence. This approach isn't just about picking the path with the highest expected value; it's about understanding the dynamics between various factors and how they influence the outcome.

The main benefit of using decision trees is that they provide a structured way to tackle decision-making. By visually laying out options, probabilities, and outcomes, they help both organizations and individuals navigate uncertainty. They enforce a meticulous way of evaluating the impact of each choice before making a decision, which is crucial in today's ever-changing world, where decisions can have significant effects.

Looking back at past uses of decision trees, their vast applicability becomes clear. For instance, the Harvard Business Review (1964) discussed their role in assisting with complex management decisions like investing in new projects or expansions. The article on Stygian Chemical Industries, Ltd. showcased decision trees in action, analyzing whether to build facilities based on market forecasts. These historical examples highlight the proven effectiveness of decision trees in strategy and decision-making.

While decision trees are beneficial, they don't give absolute answers. They clarify and structure the decision-making path, encouraging a thorough consideration of all possible outcomes.

Nonetheless, the success of decision trees largely depends on the accuracy of the information fed into them. Therefore, while they are great for organizing and visualizing decisions, it's vital to examine the data and assumptions they're based on critically. Data reliability involves checking sources, seeking expert advice, and revising assumptions with new insights.

Adopting decision trees provides businesses and individuals with a robust framework for making decisions. Whether dealing with strategic investment, operational shifts, or everyday challenges, the clarity gained from exploring different options and outcomes can be transformative. It enables well-informed risk-taking, resource optimization, and alignment with our objectives and values.

Strategic Tools for Enhanced Decision-Making

This book section explored several essential techniques, such as SWOT analysis, Cost-Benefit Analysis, Scenario Planning, and Decision Trees. These techniques are great tools for making smarter strategic choices. They help businesses identify risks, spot opportunities, and clarify priorities when the market changes.

First, we talked about how critical it is to know your company's strong points and weak spots and the chances and challenges out in the world using SWOT analysis. Then, we looked at cost-benefit analysis, which helps us understand a decision's financial pros and cons. We also discussed Scenario Planning, which prepares us for the future. Finally, we introduced Decision Trees, which help break down complicated decisions into something easier to understand.

As we try to find our way through the complex field of business strategy, these methods are more than just helpful hints. They're the solid base that makes informed, strong decision-making possible. They show us that even when things are uncertain, having a systematic way to look at choices can point us toward success.

The real test is knowing how to use these strategies smartly. They're not perfect answers but guides that need us to think critically and adapt them to fit the situation. As the business world keeps changing, developing a strategy-focused mindset is crucial. It turns potential roadblocks into opportunities that push us closer to our goals.

References

Alliance For Decision Education. (2023). *Using A Decision Tree to Drive a Decision*. Alliance for Decision Education. Retrieved from https://alliancefordecisioneducation.org/resources/using-a-decision-tree-to-drive-a-decision/

Econlib. (2021). *Decision Making and Cost-Benefit Analysis*. Retrieved from https://www.econlib.org/library/Topics/HighSchool/DecisionMakingCostBenefitAnalysis.html

Edge, D. (2021). *The role of cost-benefit analysis in public policy decision-making. Berkeley Public Policy Journal*. Retrieved from https://bppj.studentorg.berkeley.edu/2021/12/14/the-role-of-cost-benefit-analysis-in-public-policy-decision-making/

Enterprise Risk Management Initiative. (2024). *ERM Tool: Understanding the Organization's Core Strategic Drivers. Enterprise Risk Management Initiative.* Retrieved from https://erm.ncsu.edu/resource-center/erm-tool-understanding-the-organizations-core-strategic-drivers/

Harvard Business Review. (1964). *Decision trees for decision-making. Harvard Business Review.* 364(7). https://hbr.org/1964/07/decision-trees-for-decision-making

Harvard Business School Online. (2019). *Cost-Benefit Analysis: What it is & How to Do It. Business Insights Blog.* Retrieved from https://online.hbs.edu/blog/post/cost-benefit-analysis

SSIR.. (n.d.). *Using Scenario Planning to Surface Invisible Risks (SSIR).* https://ssir.org/articles/entry/using_scenario_planning_to_surface_invisible_risks

Song, Y., & Lu, Y. (2015). *Decision tree methods: applications for classification and prediction. Shanghai Archives of Psychiatry*, 27(2), 130. https://doi.org/10.11919/j.issn.1002-0829.215044

The Strategy Institute. (n.d.). *SWOT Analysis: How to Strengthen Your Business Plan.* Retrieved from https://www.thestrategyinstitute.org/insights/swot-analysis-how-to-strengthen-your-business-plan

U.S. Economic Development Administration. (n.d.). *SWOT Analysis*. Retrieved from https://www.eda.gov/resources/comprehensive-economic-development-strategy/content/swot-analysis

Waldron, L., & Searle, B. (2022). *Making sense of uncertainty: Nonprofit scenario planning*. Retrieved from https://www.bridgespan.org/insights/nonprofit-organizational-effectiveness/making-sense-of-uncertainty-nonprofit-scenario-planning

Data-Driven Decision-Making Strategies

In today's digital age, the skill to navigate through vast amounts of data to find valuable insights is crucial for companies that want to stay ahead of the competition. This need has made strategies based on data-driven decisions go from being a bonus to an absolute necessity in business environments worldwide. With the appropriate tools and knowledge, businesses can leverage data analysis and prediction methods, turning simple figures into plans that guide them toward more stable and prosperous futures.

The real challenge, however, isn't just collecting the data but understanding what it tells us. The overwhelming amount of data available can lead to hesitation, where decisions get postponed or not made because of the worry about making wrong inferences from the data. Moreover, the quick changes in market conditions and consumer preferences require companies to be responsive and predictively proactive. This means they must consistently collect, examine, and act on data, which becomes more complicated without proper methods and tools.

Leveraging Statistical Models for Predictive Analytics

Predictive analytics, which relies on statistical models, is at the core of making intelligent business decisions. These tools are fantastic for combing through large amounts of data to find patterns and predict future events, making them essential in a world heavily relying on data. But why are they so crucial for companies wanting to stay competitive? Let's explore this topic further.

Statistical models act as a connector between raw data and meaningful conclusions. They help interpret complex datasets, allowing businesses to foresee upcoming trends and behaviors. This is not just about using past and current data; it's about creating a precise forecast of the future with remarkable precision. Employing statistical models to identify trends enables companies to shift from guesswork to accurate predictions. Beyond forecasting, these models also support businesses moving from a reactive way of making decisions—often based on gut feeling or previous experiences—to a proactive approach rooted in data-driven insight.

Consider a retail company that uses past sales data, customer preferences, and market trends to predict future product demand. Such forecasts can help manage inventory more effectively, reduce excess stock, and satisfy consumer demands efficiently. The insights gained from statistical modeling help companies make well-informed choices, avoiding the common pitfalls of over- or under-preparation that come with decision-making without solid data analysis.

However, the adoption of statistical models presents its challenges and requirements. For businesses to benefit fully from these tools, it's vital to:

- Collect high-quality, relevant data since the accuracy of predictions made by statistical models depends mainly on the data fed into them.

- Choose a suitable model tailored to the specific analytical needs and objectives. Different models exist for varied prediction and analysis purposes.

- Regularly update and fine-tune the models to keep pace with evolving trends and data patterns, requiring ongoing testing with new data sets for performance assessment and adjustments.

- Provide training for team members to boost their skills in using statistical tools and interpreting the results correctly.

Statistical models also play a crucial role in risk assessment and scenario planning, allowing businesses to consider possible future events and their outcomes ("What Is Statistical Modeling?", n.d.). This is particularly valuable in today's volatile markets, where risks can appear suddenly. By examining different economic indicators and market trends, companies can prepare for various scenarios, such as economic downturns, changes in consumer habits, or supply chain issues. Being prepared allows organizations to create backup plans, reducing the potential impact of risks.

Furthermore, statistical models' benefits go beyond predicting sales or understanding customer behavior; they are also invaluable in evaluating financial risks, improving operations, and guiding strategic investments. By quantifying uncertainties and assessing the likelihood of different outcomes, companies can make well-thought-out decisions that match their long-term goals and risk tolerance.

Additionally, adopting statistical models promotes an informed decision-making culture within an organization. It shifts the focus from gut instinct or top-down decisions to a collective approach where choices are backed up by hard evidence and thorough analysis. This change improves the accuracy of decisions and increases transparency and accountability, empowering employees at every level.

Interpreting Data Trends for Strategic Insights

Understanding data trends goes beyond just staring at figures in a spreadsheet. It's really about grasping what these numbers say about potential business opportunities and their potential hazards. Imagine it as putting together a jigsaw puzzle, with each piece of data adding to our understanding of the broader market scenario. This approach provides businesses with the insights needed for making wise decisions, helping them to spot chances for growth or warning signs before any trouble gets too severe.

As the marketplace changes, businesses must also adjust their strategies accordingly. Grasping data trends helps companies remain agile, tweaking their methods as market conditions shift. This isn't just about reacting after the fact; it's about being one step ahead. By monitoring these trends closely, companies can prepare for upcoming shifts rather than playing catch-up. Being adaptable is key in today's quick-moving world, where being ahead can make the difference between flourishing and just getting by.

Taking full advantage of emerging trends requires action, not just awareness. Here are steps organizations can take to not only spot but also effectively use these trends for their benefit:

- Regularly check your data for accuracy, ensuring decisions are based on current information.

- Create a workplace that values creativity and new ideas by capitalizing on these trends for business improvement.

- Offer training for employees to boost their data analysis and interpretation skills, allowing your company to fully benefit from what the data reveals.

Furthermore, translating data trends into predictive models is a game-changer for strategic planning. These models use past data to predict future situations, offering businesses a glimpse into what could happen based on different strategies. This foresight is golden, making it possible for firms to plan with more assurance. Creating strong predictive models involves understanding the data deeply and considering external factors that might affect its reliability. To develop these models, organizations should:

- Gather diverse datasets that cover various factors impacting their market.

- Apply advanced statistical methods to sift through this data, spotting patterns that hint at future trends.

- Update these models regularly with fresh data and results to keep them accurate and relevant.

The importance of weaving data analysis and forecasting into business strategy is enormous. A study by PwC showed that companies focused on data are three times more likely to achieve significant decision-making improvements than those who don't emphasize data (HBS Online, 2019). This finding highlights the critical role of data in shaping strategic decisions, suggesting that thriving in today's business world depends on interpreting and acting on data-derived insights.

Enhancing Decision Clarity with Data Visualization

Data visualization is a game-changer in making decisions, particularly in business. It simplifies complex data into clear graphs and charts, making it easy for organizations to sift through vast information. This way, crucial decisions are based on solid analysis instead of guesses. The key is to break down complex data into visuals that quickly get the point across, leading to more intelligent decision-making. Here's how you can do this:

- First, pinpoint the essential data that influences your decisions.
- Choose visualization tools that fit your needs and can handle your data's complexity.
- Create your visuals to spotlight the most critical information clearly and concisely.
- Try your visualizations with people from varying backgrounds to ensure everyone can understand them.

One of the most significant benefits of data visualization is its ability to reveal trends and anomalies that might not be obvious otherwise. Through visual aids, businesses clearly understand where they stand and see trends over time, helping predict future shifts and adjust strategies as needed. Spotting these trends and anomalies leads to more informed, strategic choices by uncovering potential challenges and opportunities that might have been missed using traditional data analysis techniques. To spot these effectively, you should:

- Use various visualizations, like line graphs or heat maps, to show different data aspects.

- Apply colors and other cues to identify critical patterns or differences.

- Add interactive features that let people dig deeper into the data.

- Keep your visualizations up-to-date with the latest data and insights.

Moreover, data visualization tools significantly improve how vital information is shared with stakeholders. These tools offer a platform for showcasing data in an easy-to-grasp way, sparking engaging discussions about the findings. Choosing the right tools involves considering what your organization needs and what your team can handle technically. Opt for tools that balance advanced analytics with ease of use, catering to a broad audience.

Interestingly, not all aspects of data visualization require strict guidelines. For example, it naturally supports teamwork by providing a common visual reference that aids in discussions, debates, and agreements. This approach fosters unity through open communication facilitated by shared visuals.

Yet, while data visualization has many perks, it demands critical thinking and caution. Not every visualization is reliable; some can mislead, leading to incorrect conclusions. Therefore, it's crucial to scrutinize the data's source, methodology, and presentation. Ensuring that visualizations accurately represent the data and convey the right message requires attention to detail and a commitment to honesty (Torkildson, 2024).

Expanding beyond business, data visualization also plays a significant role in societal decision-making. By supporting policies backed by solid evidence and pushing for data-driven reforms, we can tackle health care, education, and housing issues more effectively. Data visualization transforms raw data into impactful stories that can shift public opinion and shape policy decisions. Valuing empirical evidence and striving to balance economic growth and welfare, I view data visualization as essential for delivering persuasive data presentations.

Implementing Machine Learning for Predictive Modeling

Machine learning is revolutionizing how we analyze data, providing businesses with the tools to predict future events accurately. These algorithms can spot patterns and trends by analyzing vast historical and real-time data sets. This insight isn't just about peering into a crystal ball for future predictions; it's about making smarter choices now to pave the way for success down the line. For companies keen on harnessing machine learning for better forecasts, there's a path lined with several vital steps.

The first step involves gathering and preparing the data, which lays the groundwork for any machine learning endeavor. It's crucial to clean this data, organizing it neatly while tossing out unnecessary bits and fixing gaps. Achieving top-notch data quality involves:

- Pulling together data from various sources to broaden your dataset.
- Carefully cleaning the data to eliminate errors and duplicates.
- Standardizing the data format through normalization to ensure consistency across the board.

Next is selecting the most suitable machine learning algorithm for the task. The choice depends on the type of data you're dealing with and the outcome you aim to predict. While some algorithms are adept at uncovering complex patterns in large datasets, others might be more effective for forecasting based on sequential data. The trick lies in experimenting with different algorithms and adjusting their settings for the best results.

After picking and training the correct algorithm, machine learning can take the reins of decision-making, offering significant time and resource savings (Roller, 2023). In practical terms, machines, rather than humans, can make quick, accurate decisions on routine matters. For example, they could automatically tweak inventory levels according to predicted demand or tailor marketing efforts to each customer without needing a person to oversee every step.

But the perks of machine learning go beyond just streamlining and speeding up processes. These algorithms are capable of evolving as they digest new data. Given how rapidly business landscapes can shift, this capacity to adapt is critical. Whereas traditional analysis methods might falter under rapid changes, machine learning models stay up-to-date, ensuring their insights remain pertinent.

Moreover, machine learning sharpens the accuracy of predictive analytics. Unlike conventional analysis, which focuses on past or present patterns, predictive modeling looks ahead, estimating future occurrences with considerable certainty. This forward-looking approach helps businesses anticipate market changes, shifts in consumer preferences, and emerging risks, enabling proactive rather than reactive strategies.

The impact of precise predictive modeling must be balanced. Imagine being able to predict when customers might leave and take steps to keep them, or analyzing social media sentiment in real time to understand public perception of your brand. Such capabilities give businesses an edge and empower them to use their resources more wisely and execute their plans with greater assurance.

However, integrating machine learning into business workflows does pose challenges, such as finding skilled professionals to develop and manage these systems and maintaining the integrity of the underlying data. Despite these hurdles, the benefits for business decision-making are clear-cut.

Predictive modeling is reshaping decision-making across industries, offering insights once deemed unreachable. With ongoing advancements in machine learning technology, its influence on business strategy and efficiency is set to escalate. Looking ahead, businesses' ability to leverage these sophisticated algorithms for interpreting complex data and uncovering valuable insights will be paramount.

Staying ahead with machine learning and predictive modeling demands keeping up with tech advancements and building a culture that values informed decision-making. As digital dependency grows, mastering machine learning becomes crucial for thriving in the digital era.

Key takeaways: Understanding statistical models, data trends, data visualization, and machine learning is essential for businesses to enhance their decision-making capabilities. Leveraging these data-driven techniques can lead to more informed, proactive, and strategic choices that align with organizational goals and drive success.

Grasping the concepts of statistical models, understanding data trends, and making the most of data visualization and machine learning are crucial for businesses looking to improve their decisions. Employing these data-centric approaches can help companies make smart, forward-thinking choices that align with their overall objectives, paving the way for success.

Throughout this chapter, we've delved into the power of data analysis and forecasting as tools to boost business decision-making processes. Starting from the basics of statistical models for predicting future scenarios, we've moved on to deciphering data trends for valuable insights, emphasizing the importance of using data visualization to make complex information more accessible and discussing adopting machine learning for more accurate predictions. Together, these elements offer a solid foundation for businesses striving to stay ahead in the competitive market by making well-informed decisions.

We are reflecting on our starting point, and it seems that the blend of technology and data science opens up new avenues for businesses to foresee what's coming and shape their future favorably. Embracing these advanced techniques might present challenges, but it gives organizations the necessary resources to take dynamic, informed actions.

Transitioning from theoretical concepts to real-world applications underscores the critical role that data analysis plays in formulating a business strategy. It's a journey that begins with gathering quality data and extends to utilizing cutting-edge machine learning algorithms, signifying a dedication to nurturing an innovative, evidence-oriented decision-making culture within companies.

References

Brightspot, E. (2023). *How Data Science Drives Business Decision-Making. Unlocking Business Success: The Role of Data Science*. Retrieved from https://online.mason.wm.edu/blog/how-data-science-drives-business-decision-making

Coursera. (n.d.). *Statistical modeling is like a formal depiction of a theory. It is typically described as the mathematical relationship between random and non-random variables*. Retrieved from https://www.coursera.org/articles/statistical-modeling

Emeritus Online Courses. (2024). *Predictive Modeling: The Ultimate Guide to Unlock Hidden Profits. Emeritus Online Courses.* Retrieved from https://emeritus.org/blog/what-is-predictive-modeling/

HBS Online. (2019). *The Advantages of Data-Driven Decision-Making. Business Insights Blog.* Retrieved from https://online.hbs.edu/blog/post/data-driven-decision-making

Harvard Business School Online. (2019). *The advantages of data-driven decision-making. Business Insights Blog.* Retrieved from https://online.hbs.edu/blog/post/data-driven-decision-making

IABAC, alagar. (2024). *The Role of Predictive Analytics in Decision Making.* IABAC®. Retrieved from https://iabac.org/blog/the-role-of-predictive-analytics-in-decision-making

Michigan Technological University. (2021). *Why is Statistics Important in Decision-Making?.* Retrieved from https://onlinedegrees.mtu.edu/news/why-statistics-important-decision-making

OnlineDegrees, SCU. (2023). *Strategies for Making Data-Driven Decisions.* Onlinedegrees.scu. https://onlinedegrees.scu.edu/media/blog/strategies-for-making-data-driven-decisions

Padilla, L. M., Creem-Regehr, S. H., Hegarty, M., & Stefanucci, J. K. (2018). *Decision making with visualizations: A cognitive framework across disciplines.* Cognitive Research: Principles and Implications, 3(10). https://doi.org/10.1186/s41235-018-0120-9

Roller, J. (2023). *4 Growing Machine Learning Use Cases For Business. IEEE Computer Society.* Retrieved from https://www.computer.org/publications/tech-news/trends/business-case-for-machine-learning/

Torkildson, A. (2024). *I am visualizing Data for Informed Decision-Making. SCORE.* Retrieved from https://www.score.org/utah/resource/blog-post/visualizing-data-informed-decision-making

William & Mary. (2023). *How Data Science Drives Business Decision-Making.* Retrieved from https://online.mason.wm.edu/blog/how-data-science-drives-business-decision-making

Risk Mitigation and Opportunity Seizure

Being a strong leader and a strategic thinker is crucial for successfully navigating the ever-changing business world. Imagine the business world as a vast ocean filled with potential storms and golden opportunities. A well-prepared business can sail through difficulties and grab onto opportunities for growth that come its way. Balancing risk management with seizing opportunities is at the heart of savvy decision-making.

Central to every decision in the business arena is dealing with uncertainty. Market, technology, or customer preference changes can throw a wrench in the most well-laid plans. Facing these uncertainties may feel like trying to find your way through thick fog, with each step needing careful thought to avoid hidden dangers. Yet, it's within this uncertainty that opportunities lie. These opportunities demand quick thinking and the ability to spot them amidst the chaos. Thus, the challenge isn't just about dodging risks but also being ready to leap when the right moment presents itself.

Introducing Risk Mitigation Strategies

In the ever-changing landscape of business, one thing is sure: risks come with the territory. Instead of seeing these risks merely as hurdles, it's more useful to view them as chances to strengthen and improve our decision-making. With this mindset, let's explore some innovative strategies to help us avoid pitfalls while creating opportunities for unexpected successes.

Starting, let's talk about spreading out your investments. Think of it like not putting all your eggs in one basket. When you spread out your investments across different types of assets, you're less likely to feel the sting if one investment doesn't perform well. This makes your overall portfolio more stable and capable of navigating through ups and downs in the market. To do this right, you should examine your current investments and see where you can bring variety to balance things. Keeping an eye on how your diversified portfolio performs and adjusting as needed is critical to keeping your investments healthy.

Then, there's the technique called scenario planning. This method helps you think about different future outcomes, from the most likely to the most outlandish, and how they could affect your business. It's like having a game plan ready, no matter what the future throws at you. By understanding potential challenges and opportunities ahead of time, businesses can develop flexible and responsive strategies. Start by figuring out what external factors impact your business, imagine several possible futures based on these factors, and plan how to navigate each scenario.

Moving forward, I would like to point out that having a backup or contingency plan is critical. These plans are your playbook for dealing with unexpected events to keep your business running smoothly. Putting together effective contingency plans starts with pinpointing the essential parts of your business and the risks that could throw them off track. Once you know the risks, you can create detailed plans to tackle each.

Keeping these plans up to date and practicing them regularly ensures they work when needed.

Lastly, continuously monitoring risks is crucial. This means setting up systems that constantly check for and assess new risks, allowing you to deal with them before they become more significant problems. This forward-looking approach is about avoiding trouble and finding new ways to grow and innovate. Setting up risk monitoring involves putting processes in place for regular check-ups, using tech to streamline data gathering, and ensuring straightforward ways to communicate and act fast when situations arise.

By embracing these strategies—diversifying investments, planning for various scenarios, preparing contingency plans, and continuously monitoring risks—businesses can withstand uncertainties and flourish amidst them. These methods highlight the importance of proactive risk management rather than merely reacting when issues emerge. As Kaplan et al. (2012) cleverly note, recognizing the differences between risks can help manage management practices effectively, ensuring that protective measures and growth opportunities are maximized.

Identifying Opportunities Through Market Analysis

Unlocking the potential of untapped market opportunities starts with a deep dive into the competitive arena. More than simply putting out a new product or service is required. You need to carefully study what's already out there, spot any unmet needs, and consider how upcoming trends could influence what consumers want. This kind of strategic thinking doesn't just happen by chance; it requires a detailed analysis of your competitors. Here's a down-to-earth way to go about it:

- First up, figure out who you're competing against. Break them into groups: those you're up against right now, those who might not be in your space but could be soon, and those who could become competitors.

- Dive into everything they offer, how they market themselves, what their customers think of them, and their overall financial well-being to grasp their strong suits and weak spots.

- Keep an eye out for any patterns in what they do that might show opportunities they've missed.

- Always stay alert to any changes in their game plan, which might hint at broader shifts in the market or new chances for you to jump on.

Understanding what the people you're aiming to serve want is critical. In today's fast-changing world, where customer loyalty is never a given, getting a handle on your target audience's shifting tastes and requirements is critical. This means:

- Directly contacting customers via surveys, interviews, and other ways to hear from them.

- Looking at market research reports and insights into consumer trends to forecast where things are heading.

- Keeping your buyer personas fresh to reflect changes in how consumers act or what they prefer.

A SWOT analysis - which looks at Strengths, Weaknesses, Opportunities, and Threats - is essential for knowing where your business stands and maximizing your internal strengths while dealing with external challenges. To pull off a solid SWOT analysis:

- Note down the strengths and weaknesses within your business, focusing on what resources, abilities, and processes you have.

- Spot external opportunities and threats by examining what's happening in the market, what your competitors are up to, and any regulatory shifts.

- Use this insight to prioritize strategic moves, aiming to maximize strengths and opportunities while minimizing weaknesses and safeguarding against threats.

Having systems in place to learn from real-world results and customer feedback is vital for tweaking strategies as needed. Setting up effective feedback loops includes:

- Creating ways for customers to share their thoughts with you, such as surveys, social media conversations, and reviews of your products.

- Fostering a culture of open communication in your company so that insights from staff who deal directly with customers can come to light.

- Consistently review feedback and let it guide your strategy sessions to keep your business in line with what customers seek.

By embracing these strategies, companies can put themselves in a solid position to spot and seize new opportunities. Taking a proactive approach to strategizing allows for more innovative risks and better-informed decisions. As Marcel Planellas explains in "The 3-stage Process for Making Strategic Decisions," striking the right balance between analyzing, deciding, and implementing is crucial, with every choice guided by the organization's core purpose, ambitions, and principles (The 3-stage Process for making strategic decisions, n.d.). Adopting this mindset gives businesses the skills to effectively tackle market challenges, ensuring they survive and excel in the face of competition.

Digging into these strategic practices gives organizations the tools to chart a course grounded in the current market situation and flexible enough for future shifts. The business world constantly changes, marked by rapid tech advancements, evolving customer preferences, and unpredictable economic scenarios. With this backdrop, being able to spot areas for growth through meticulous market analysis is invaluable for any business keen on staying ahead.

Exploring markets for opportunities goes beyond just edging out competitors; it lays the groundwork for a resilient business model that endures through ups and downs and ever-changing market dynamics. By focusing on these strategic paths, businesses signal their dedication to their success and to contributing positively to the larger ecosystem, acknowledging that true advancement originates from a nuanced understanding and adaptation to our collective surroundings.

This approach highlights the fluid relationship between businesses and their environments, emphasizing the need for ongoing alertness and adaptability. It reminds us that in the corporate sphere, standing still equates to falling behind. Thus, embracing a structured approach to decision-making rooted in comprehensive market analysis is more than a strategic option—it's essential for lasting achievement.

Seizing Competitive Advantages

Getting a leg up in the competitive business world requires more than keeping an eye on rivals. It's about constantly finding new ways to improve by inventing new products and improving your processes, services, and business practices. This calls for an open-minded approach, always looking for chances to enhance every part of your operation. The key is encouraging your team to develop fresh, innovative ideas and building an environment where such creativity is appreciated and taken seriously.

Moreover, the importance of forming strategic partnerships must be considered. Working with others who bring different yet complementary strengths can amplify what you can achieve independently. These alliances can help broaden your reach in the market, provide access to new customer groups or technologies, and much more. Communicating is crucial to establishing and keeping these valuable relationships strong and setting out everyone's goals and what you expect from the partnership. Here are a few steps to guide you in cultivating meaningful collaborations:

- Look for potential partners who offer strengths that complement yours and share similar values.

- Make sure all involved understand what you aim to achieve together.

- Maintain open communication and regular catch-ups to stay on the same track.

- Evaluate the success of the collaboration and be willing to tweak roles and expectations as things progress.

Another cornerstone of maintaining a competitive edge is aligning your pricing strategies with the value customers believe they're getting. It's essential that customers feel your product or service is worth paying a bit more for compared to cheaper alternatives. This involves identifying which features of your offering are most valued by your customers and making sure these are front and center in your marketing efforts. Your prices should reflect your product or service's unique benefits and value, adopting a value-based pricing approach. This might mean doing extensive market research to grasp how your customers view your offerings and what they're willing to pay.

Being adaptable and agile is increasingly critical in today's fast-paced business environment. The ability to quickly pivot in response to market changes gives companies a notable edge over their competition. Creating a culture that values flexibility and quick decision-making can make all the difference in seizing new opportunities or being left behind. This means promoting a mindset that welcomes change across the organization and simplifying how decisions are made to act fast.

Investing in the right technology and training and providing your team with the tools to innovate and adjust proactively is also vital.

When you weave these strategies together—innovation, strategic partnerships, innovative pricing, and organizational agility—you create a solid framework capable of surviving and thriving under competitive pressures. Standing out through continuous innovation, working closely with the right partners, setting prices based on the value perceived by customers, and maintaining an agile company culture are critical ingredients for sustained growth and leadership in the market. A point emphasized in the Harvard Business Review is that leading companies set themselves apart by evolving planning into strategic management. This revitalizes complex businesses, ensuring they stay at the forefront of their industry long-term (Harvard Business Review, 1980).

Adapting to Market Uncertainties with Agility

In the world of business, smoothly riding through the unexpected ups and downs of the market is a clear sign of an organization's strength and smart planning. It's not just about making quick decisions on the fly; it's about having a deep-seated strategy that embraces flexibility at its core. Let's explore how businesses can stay nimble and sharp-eyed in this ever-changing environment.

Starting with scenario planning is critical for nurturing this kind of adaptability. This strategy lets businesses paint a picture of future scenarios, ranging from best-case to worst-case situations. Here are some actionable steps:

- Start with picturing different futures that could unfold.

- Identify the significant factors that might steer these scenarios in one direction or another and monitor them closely.

- Craft specific plans for each possible outcome to ensure you're always one step ahead.

Scenario planning serves as a guide during uncertain times, steering decision-making towards being proactive rather than reactive, as noted by Chevallier (2021). This method does more than prepare companies for what lies ahead; it instills a culture that values forward-thinking and adaptability.

Fostering an experimental culture is equally important. Innovation is nurtured in places that welcome trial and error, viewing failures as lessons rather than defeats. To create such an environment:

- Make it safe for team members to suggest and try out new ideas without fearing negative consequences if they fail.

- Set up a system for feedback so every experiment, successful or not, becomes a learning opportunity.

- Honor both victories and valuable mistakes to emphasize the importance of progress and learning.

This ongoing cycle of testing, learning, and improving creates an ideal setting for innovation and adaptability, which are crucial for dealing with uncertain market conditions.

Promoting teamwork across different business functions also breaks barriers and boosts problem-solving skills. When teams from various backgrounds work together, they bring unique perspectives and abilities that lead to more intelligent, flexible decision-making. Here's how to enhance this collaboration:

- Form cross-functional teams for particular projects, giving them specific goals and the freedom to achieve them.

- Use tools and platforms that make working together easier, breaking down communication hurdles.

- Schedule regular meetings with people from different departments to share insights, challenges, and opportunities, building a sense of unity and shared vision.

Such teamwork speeds up the decision-making process and adds depth to it with varied viewpoints, helping the organization adjust quickly to changes.

Lastly, leveraging technology and data is crucial for making faster and more accurate decisions. In our digital era, data is vital, offering insights that significantly cut down uncertainties. To make the most of technology and data:

- Invest in tools that provide up-to-the-minute data and forecasts.

- Teach your team how to use this data in their decision-making.

- Build a culture where decisions are based on complex data rather than just gut feelings.

By tapping into technology and data, companies can edge out competition, making well-informed decisions swiftly and accurately.

When we combine these strategies—scenario planning, creating an experimental mindset, boosting cross-functional teamwork, and utilizing technology and data—businesses can turn uncertainty into a field ripe with possibilities. This readiness not only prepares organizations for upcoming challenges but also sets them up to take advantage of new opportunities in a shifting marketplace.

Today's volatile business climate requires moving from strict, inflexible plans to adaptable, dynamic strategies. As Chevallier (2021) points out, agility in decision-making helps leaders better tackle the complexities of today's market, allowing for swift adjustments as needed. With an all-encompassing, flexible approach to decision-making, companies can maintain continuity, achieve growth, and remain strong, no matter how unpredictable the market gets.

Reflecting on these strategies, the real power of adaptability doesn't come from foretelling the future with perfect accuracy but from being fully prepared for its many twists and turns. In a world of constant change, the capacity to adapt swiftly and strategically is crucial for lasting success. Businesses that embrace these flexible decision-making practices can confidently move through uncertainty, transforming potential challenges into chances for growth and innovation.

Enhancing Decision-Making Processes

In wrapping up our discussion, we've taken a thorough journey through minimizing risks and grasping opportunities by making strategic decisions. The core takeaway from our conversations is acknowledging the dangers and chances every business encounters and implementing an organized strategy to handle these challenges. Initially, we highlighted the significance of spreading out investments, planning for various future scenarios, preparing backup plans, and keeping a vigilant eye on potential risks as critical components to maintaining a resilient business.

Digging deeper into the marketplace analysis, we discovered how crucial it is to spot potential opportunities by understanding the competitive landscape deeply and swiftly adapting to changes in consumer preferences and market dynamics. Furthermore, harnessing competitive edges through creativity, forming strategic alliances, applying value-oriented pricing, and enhancing organizational flexibility were pinpointed as vital strategies to outmaneuver competitors and secure long-term progress.

Standing at this point in our dialogue, it becomes evident that managing risks while recognizing opportunities involves a delicate mix of meticulous planning and flexible implementation. These insights act as navigational tools for busy professionals navigating their enterprises through unpredictable conditions, pointing the way toward more secure and thriving futures.

References

Bourgeois, L. (1980). *Strategic management for competitive advantage*. Harvard Business Review, 3804. Retrieved from https://hbr.org/1980/07/strategic-management-for-competitive-advantage

Coursera. (n.d.). *Market Analysis: What It Is and How to Conduct One*. Retrieved from https://www.coursera.org/articles/market-analysis

Coursera. (n.d.). *What Is Competitive Advantage and How to Find Your Strategic Edge*. Retrieved from https://www.coursera.org/articles/competitive-advantage

Eisenhardt, K. M. (1999). *Strategy as Strategic Decision Making. MIT Sloan Management Review*. Retrieved from https://sloanreview.mit.edu/article/strategy-as-strategic-decision-making/

Ellsworth, L. (2021). *Making decisions in the face of uncertainty. I by IMD*. Retrieved from https://www.imd.org/ibyimd/brain-circuits/making-decisions-in-the-face-of-uncertainty/

Harvard Business Review. (2020). *An Agile Approach to Budgeting for Uncertain Times*. Retrieved from https://hbr.org/2020/08/an-agile-approach-to-budgeting-for-uncertain-times

ISACA. (2021). *Using Risk Assessment to Support Decision Making*. ISACA. https://www.isaca.org/resources/news-and-trends/industry-news/2021/using-risk-assessment-to-support-decision-making

Kaplan, R. S., & Mikes, A. (2012). *Managing risks: A new framework. Harvard Business Review.* https://hbr.org/2012/06/managing-risks-a-new-framework

National Academies of Sciences, Engineering, and Medicine. (2021). *The Owner's Role in Project Risk Management.* The National Academies Press. https://doi.org/10.17226/11183

There is no author information available. ("n.d."). *The 3-stage process for making strategic decisions. ESADE Knowledge.* They were retrieved from https://dobetter.esade.edu/en/making-strategic-decisions.

University of Michigan Ross School of Business. (n.d.). *Strategic Decision Making.* Retrieved from https://michiganross.umich.edu/programs/executive-education/strategic-decision-making

Strategic Decision-Making in Real-World Scenarios

In today's fast-paced business environment, making savvy strategic decisions is more crucial than ever. Businesses find themselves at critical junctures, weighing whether to venture into new markets, introduce new products, or shift strategies in light of unexpected challenges. These choices are pivotal, marking the path to triumph for some and decline for others. Looking closely at how giants like Nestle and Coca-Cola strategically entered emerging markets sheds light on the importance of making well-informed decisions. It clearly illustrates the complex interplay between decision-making and its outcomes that dominate the business world.

Navigating the journey towards these critical decisions comes with its share of hurdles. Enterprises face many challenges - from getting to grips with the subtleties of foreign markets and dealing with the shocks of technological upheaval to rethinking their core activities during economic strain. Each situation requires not just any response but a carefully crafted strategy that looks ahead, considering the immediate results and future implications. The real difficulty often doesn't stem from a lack of data but rather from the challenge of molding this wealth of information into valuable insights. Companies struggle to sift through the clutter to pinpoint what's essential, striking a balance between risk and potential gain, all while making timely decisions that keep pace with the ever-evolving market landscape.

Applying Strategic Decision-Making Through Case Studies

When we dive into strategic decision-making, it's clear that making informed decisions matters. How companies decide to enter new markets is a great way to understand this better. A compelling case study highlighted by Greer (2018) examines how big names like Nestle, Coca-Cola, PepsiCo, and Pizza Hut moved into India's growing food and beverage sector. These companies showed how crucial it is to do your homework on the market and choose the best way to enter it—whether through exporting goods, setting up their branches, partnering with local companies, or franchising. Each option has its ups and downs, but these successful brands shared one thing: they all thoroughly researched and got to know the local scene.

To make your way through such intricate situations, here are some smart moves to consider:

- Dive deep into a PESTEL analysis to get the big picture of the political, economic, social, technological, environmental, and legal landscapes.

- Use Porter's Five Forces to gauge the competition level and attractiveness of the industry.

- Pick an entry strategy that matches your strengths and goals while being mindful of potential hurdles.

- Stay flexible, always ready to fine-tune your approach based on what you're hearing from the market and any new developments.

As we shift our focus from entering markets to navigating tough decisions within them, the spotlight falls on the need for businesses to be resilient and adapt. There are many stories of companies facing unexpected challenges yet managing not just to hold on but to come out ahead by cleverly changing direction. These scenarios underscore that making a strategic choice isn't a one-and-done deal; it's about continuously evaluating and adjusting. Although there might not be a step-by-step guide for these situations, the takeaway is clear: resilience and adaptability are vital in strategic decision-making.

Embracing failures as learning opportunities is another important aspect of improving decision-making abilities. It's a stark reminder that, despite careful planning and anticipation, things don't always go as expected. The insights gained from these setbacks are precious, shedding light on factors we might have missed, the role of timing, and, sometimes, how unpredictable markets can be. Reflecting on these experiences helps individuals and organizations become more alert and proactive in decision-making.

Applying the lessons learned from both successes and failures is key to making better strategic decisions. This involves finding the right mix of detailed analysis and intuitive thinking. For example, risk assessment tools and frameworks can help evaluate options by measuring uncertainties and potential outcomes. Moreover, creating a workplace that values fact-based decisions, promotes open discussions, and supports taking well-thought-out risks can significantly boost a company's strategic planning skills.

To enhance your decision-making, consider these best practices:

- Integrate data analytics into your decision-making to base choices on solid facts rather than just gut feelings.

- Build an environment that encourages transparency and learning from every positive or negative outcome, allowing for deeper insights.

- Continuously refresh your decision-making tools and frameworks to stay updated with market trends, technological innovations, and organizational shifts.

Navigating the complex and uncertain path of strategic decision-making can be daunting, yet following these principles and practices dramatically improves a company's navigation skills in unpredictable markets. Blending thorough analysis, strategic agility, lessons from past mistakes, and commitment to best practices lays a strong foundation for effective decision-making. Whether breaking into new territories or tackling internal challenges, the essence lies in the dynamic combination of strategies, constantly refined through experience and insight.

Strategic Decision-Making Across Various Business Contexts

Exploring strategic decision-making across different industries is quite captivating. Companies skillfully maneuver through their particular environments, aiming for success. This wide variety, from tech firms and retailers to manufacturers, reveals distinct approaches to tackling market demands and hurdles. Take Alibaba's story, as highlighted by (Explore The 7 Real World Examples of Effective Business Strategies, n.d.). Their journey towards becoming a giant in the online marketplace through platforms like Taobao and Tmall and their ventures into cloud computing and digital media show how critical it is to be flexible and proactive in today's business world.

A company's ability to bounce back and thrive speaks volumes about its strategic groundwork during challenging times. Such periods offer prime examples of why agility and prompt decision-making are invaluable. By examining instances when companies have weathered economic slumps or sudden market twists, we understand better the vital role that strategic planning plays in navigating rough waters. Crises call for swift adaptation and an openness to shift strategies on the fly, essential qualities for enduring success.

There's plenty to learn from best practices from successful strategic moves. Creating a strategic plan means evaluating risks, monitoring market trends, and preparing for various outcomes. Yet, at its core, this involves knowing your company's strengths and weaknesses. It's about making choices that match your competitive edge while not losing sight of potential risks. Scenario planning stands out here, enabling businesses to imagine possible scenarios and prepare accordingly. In a world entirely of uncertainties, such readiness is priceless.

Effectively putting decision-making models into practice can tremendously strengthen an organization's strategy execution. Here are some steps to consider:

- Start with a solid understanding of key decision-making frameworks, such as the SWOT analysis for identifying strengths, weaknesses, opportunities, and threats or Porter's Five Forces for examining competitive pressures.

- Customize these models so they fit your company and industry peculiarities.

- Involve team members from across the organization in the strategy process. This brings in varied perspectives and enriches the strategy formulation.

- Keep refining your strategies based on ongoing feedback and external changes. Remember, strategizing is a continual process.

Furthermore, real-world cases shared by The Strategy Institute and Yale School of Management (Top 40 Most Popular Case Studies of 2021, n.d.) underline the value of applying sophisticated strategic thinking in business. Stories like Hertz's financial restructuring and Starbucks' focus on value-driven customer relations are potent illustrations of strategic thinking. These companies navigated through tough times and seized new opportunities, setting an example for others.

In today's digitized world, using data analytics in crafting strategic decisions is incredibly impactful. The ability to collect, scrutinize, and make moves based on data insights gives businesses a notable edge. It shifts the basis of decisions from mere instincts to solid evidence. Firms leading in this domain are often more agile and better positioned to adjust to market dynamics, showcasing the effective merger of analytical depth and strategic vision.

The path to making wise strategic choices is complex but rewarding, requiring a nuanced understanding of both the internal workings and the external business climate. Learning from how businesses remain resilient during downturns, adopting best practices from market leaders, and applying decision-making theories pragmatically paves the way forward. This holistic approach equips companies to face current challenges and smoothly sail through future uncertainties. Cultivating a culture where decisions are grounded on facts rather than just gut feelings is equally important. These decisions should aim to fulfill long-term objectives rather than solve short-term problems.

Learning from Failures to Enhance Future Decisions

Grasping the reasons behind the failure of decisions sheds light on how we can better our decision-making skills. This perspective isn't about being negative but offers a practical look to improve how we understand and take action. Often, the root cause of not-so-great decisions comes from errors in our methods or scarcity of information and our tendency to fall into mental traps without realizing it. Hammond et al. (1998) noted that recognizing these pitfalls, such as the tendency to be too confident or to seek only confirming evidence, is critical to avoiding them. These traps can trick us into overvaluing what we know, dismissing contrary information, or clinging too tightly to familiar ground, among other dangers. Recognizing these deceptive shortcuts in our thinking is the initial step in protecting ourselves against them.

Taking steps forward includes implementing ways to get feedback within our decision-making routines, which is incredibly important for fine-tuning. Think of feedback as a navigation tool that helps steer our choices toward their desired destinations by pointing out the gap between what we expected and what happened. For anyone ready to make feedback loops a part of their routine, consider the following tips:

- Make an effort to get feedback from various sources to avoid missing anything important.

- Set up specific times and ways for feedback to be shared, making sure it's relevant and prompt.

- Take time to think about the feedback you've got and use it to shape your future strategies.

- Be open to criticism, seeing it as a chance to grow rather than something personal.

Likewise, creating a culture that views mistakes as chances to learn can change how decisions are made in teams or organizations. This approach needs leaders to create a welcoming space where team members feel safe to try new things and share different opinions without worry. Such an environment supports resilience and innovation, pushing people to adapt and try new ideas. Here are ways leaders can build this kind of culture:

- Show humility by owning up to their own mistakes.

- Celebrate efforts to innovate, even if they don't always succeed.

- Ensure communication is transparent so everyone understands how decisions are made.

Furthermore, reflecting on our past experiences is like digging into a gold mine of valuable insights that can shape our upcoming choices. Spotting trends and adjusting our tactics becomes possible by looking back at what has worked or not. This reflective cycle strengthens the foundation of our decision-making skills over time. Starting this process might look like this:

- Schedule time to review the consequences of past decisions regularly.

- Record significant findings and whether your initial guesses were right or wrong.

- Update how you make choices based on what you've learned to stay in touch with reality.

Putting these strategies into practice takes persistence and focus, but the payoff in transforming decisions is enormous. They emphasize being thoughtful over going with the flow, encouraging us to adopt a more mindful, analytical approach to making choices.

Distilling Best Practices for Effective Strategic Decision-Making

Grasping the essentials of crafting effective decision-making strategies is like finding your way through an intricate yet rewarding labyrinth. To enter this labyrinth, it's essential to pinpoint our main goals, which shine like a guiding star on a night. Like setting out on any well-thought-out adventure, understanding what we aim to accomplish makes the journey more transparent and straightforward. This approach ensures that our decisions are deeply connected with our broader aims and desired results.

Once we've established these goals, deep analysis becomes our guiding light. In making decisions, it's vital to collect and closely examine relevant information, paying attention to every detail of the current situation. Skilled decision-makers don't just think about what's happening now; they also look at what could happen in the future, including their choices' possible effects. They adopt a strategic way of thinking, spotting patterns and constants amid uncertainty, leading to solutions beyond simple troubleshooting.

As we continue through this complex maze, effectively managing risks is crucial. It's important to foresee potential hurdles and prepare for them. This means evaluating potential downsides while keeping an eye on the benefits, choosing paths that decrease problems and enhance advantages. It's similar to a tightrope walker who meticulously balances risk and reward, ever mindful of the consequences of faltering.

For those looking to incorporate these strategies into their decision-making, consider these practical steps:

- Start by defining clear, reachable goals aligning with your objectives.

- Conduct an in-depth analysis of the scenario, gathering as much relevant information as possible to guide your choices.

- Thoughtfully evaluate risks, pondering over both immediate and long-term effects, and prepare for various outcomes.

These guidelines draw from Peter F. Drucker's insights in the Harvard Business Review (Harvard Business Review, 1967), emphasizing the need for strategy and broad-based thinking rather than reactive problem-solving. Adopting such methods encourages both individuals and organizations to make informed, meaningful decisions that endure over time.

Shifting focus, the importance of embracing innovation and creativity in making strategic choices is highlighted. In our rapidly changing world, often sticking to old ways isn't enough to tackle new challenges. Here, leading companies serve as beacons of inspiration. These examples show how adopting innovative, unconventional strategies can push a company ahead of its competitors, aiming to educate and inspire. This section celebrates those trailblazers who thought outside the box, demonstrating how creative thinking can drive significant change. However, it's crucial to recognize that what works for one might not suit another; the goal is to cultivate an environment that supports fresh ideas and rewards creative risk-taking.

In the discussion around balancing risks with rewards, it becomes clear that making decisions is always accompanied by uncertainties. What sets successful organizations apart is their ability to manage this delicate balance effectively. Rather than avoiding risks, they engage in thoughtful, calculated actions that reduce potential downsides while seizing opportunities. Employing risk management strategies equips them to confront challenges confidently. This careful consideration of risks versus rewards forms the foundation of individual choices and the core values of resilient and adaptive organizations.

Lastly, nurturing a mindset focused on long-term success marks the end of our exploration through the decision-making process. It highlights the role of forward-thinking and strategic planning. This part emphasizes the importance of ensuring that every decision, no matter how small, aligns with the larger objectives and mission of the organization. By promoting a culture where every choice is made with the future in mind, businesses can achieve continued growth and remain relevant in an ever-changing world.

To encourage such a mindset:

- Foster a culture that values strategic thinking over-reactive responses.

- Ensure that all decisions, whether big or small, reflect the long-term goals and principles of the organization.

- Promote ongoing learning and flexibility, allowing the decision-making process to adapt based on new knowledge and circumstances.

Essential Takeaways for Mastering Strategic Decision-Making

Exploring the complex world of strategic decision-making, we've delved into the importance of having well-informed and flexible strategies in today's rapidly changing business environment. Through examining real-life examples like Nestle and Coca-Cola's ventures in India, we've seen that viewing failures as opportunities for growth is crucial for improving decision-making skills. This discussion aims to equip professionals with the necessary tools for success.

At the outset, we emphasized the significance of thorough research and the ability to adapt to changing circumstances. It's not just about choosing the correct course; it's also about being ready to adjust your approach when conditions evolve. This combination of flexibility and a willingness to learn from every result, whether a triumph or a setback, lays the groundwork for making choices that address present difficulties and open doors to new possibilities.

This chapter targets a diverse group of professionals, indicating that the strategies covered have broad applications. Adopting these approaches can have an impact beyond individual achievements, potentially enhancing an organization's adaptability and capacity for innovation on a grand scale.

References

Bang, D., & Frith, C. D. (2017). *Making better decisions in groups*. *Royal Society Open Science*, 8(4), 10.1098/rsos.170193. https://doi.org/10.1098/rsos.170193

Bridgespan. (2020). *From Principles to Practices: Structuring Your Decision-Making Process*. Bridgespan. Retrieved from https://www.bridgespan.org/insights/decision-making-best-practices

Drucker, P. F. (1967). *The effective decision*. Harvard Business Review. Retrieved from https://hbr.org/1967/01/the-effective-decision

Greer, G. (2018). *Win in India: An Analysis of Market Entry Strategy Into India's Food and Beverage Industry*. University of Arkansas, Fayetteville. Retrieved from https://scholarworks.uark.edu/finnuht/39

HBS Working Knowledge. (n.d.). *Read Articles about Market Entry & Exit*. Retrieved from https://hbswk.hbs.edu/Pages/browse.aspx?HBSTopic=Market%20Entry%20and%20Exit

Hammond, J., Keeney, R., & Raiffa, H. (1998). *The hidden traps in decision making. Harvard Business Review*. Retrieved from https://hbr.org/1998/09/the-hidden-traps-in-decision-making-2

Harvard Business Publishing. (n.d.). *Favorite Business Case Studies*. Retrieved from https://hbsp.harvard.edu/inspiring-minds/favorite-business-case-studies

Harvard Business School Online. (2020). *5 Key Decision-Making Techniques for Managers. Business Insights Blog.*
https://online.hbs.edu/blog/post/decision-making-techniques

The Strategy Institute. (n.d.). *Explore The 7 Real World Examples of Effective Business Strategies.* Retrieved from
https://www.thestrategyinstitute.org/insights/explore-the-7-real-world-examples-of-effective-business-strategies

Whyte, G. (1991). *Decision failures: Why they occur and how to prevent them. The Executive*, 5(3), 23-31.
https://doi.org/10.2307/4165019

Yale School of Management. (2022). *Top 40 Most Popular Case Studies of 2021.* Retrieved from https://som.yale.edu/story/2022/top-40-most-popular-case-studies-2021

Aligning Decisions with Strategic Goals

Making sure your business choices match up with the big-picture goals of your company is like being the captain of a ship in rough seas. Just as the captain tweaks the sails and alters the course to stick to the planned route, leaders in the business world must do the same with their decisions. Whether large or small, these choices push the company closer to its objectives. But if there is a clear link between these daily decisions and the broader ambitions, it's easier for things to go off track, putting those goals at risk.

Businesses often run into trouble when everyday decisions don't line up with their long-term aims. This misalignment can chew up resources, let opportunities slip by, and, in the end, prevent the organization from realizing its main targets for success. In the swift current of business operations, the urgency to make quick calls can sometimes obscure the need to ensure those choices serve the company's strategic purposes. Moreover, without a systematic way to evaluate and reassess the impact of these decisions, companies might unknowingly wander off their chosen path, only realizing the deviation when it may be too late to correct course.

Setting strategic objectives for decision alignment

Getting a grip on what an organization aims to achieve is crucial for guiding it toward victory. Imagine breaking down the big picture into smaller, doable chunks. It all starts with having a clear picture of where you want your organization to stand in the future. Then, you break those big dreams into tinier goals that act like stepping stones, leading you closer to your ultimate achievement. By tackling decisions this way, leaders can make sure their choices bolster the grand plan, avoiding distraction by short-lived opportunities or pressures that don't align with where the company wants to be in the long run.

To sharpen these goals, creating key performance indicators (KPIs) is a must. Think of KPIs as lighthouses, shining light on the path to your strategic destinations through the foggy routine of daily tasks. They give you actual numbers to check how well you're doing. For example, if becoming the top dog in your market is the end game, a KPI could be hitting a particular market share by a specific time. Selecting the right KPIs—ones that genuinely mirror what success looks like for your strategy—is critical. They must be spot-on and achievable, serving as reliable markers for making intelligent choices at every company level.

However, jotting down KPIs and then shelving them until it's report card time is as helpful as sailing without a map. The business seas constantly shift, shaped by new trends, customer habits, and tech breakthroughs. That's why it's critical to regularly check up on your strategic targets and KPIs, tweaking them to fit the current business climate. This agile approach keeps the organization flexible, ready to face hurdles or grab hold of fresh opportunities while maintaining its strategic North Star.

Ensuring everyone in the organization is on the same wavelength about these strategic aims is another cornerstone. From the CEO to the newest hire, each person should grasp how their work ties into the larger objectives. This knowledge builds a shared sense of direction and drive, pushing everyone to pull together toward typical milestones. Plus, keeping communication lines wide open welcomes valuable feedback and inventive ideas, paving the way for strategies to propel the organization toward its goals. When everyone's efforts are harmonized, achieving strategic objectives becomes a concerted effort.

Here's a roadmap for aligning actions with aspirations:

- Begin by laying out the organization's game plan with tools like the Balanced Scorecard or SMART goals. This ensures everyone understands the targets immediately before diving into KPIs.

- Involve leaders and stakeholders in creating KPIs. Getting everyone on board is vital for the heartful tracking and maintenance of these benchmarks throughout the organization (Harlow, n.d.).

- Choose KPIs that matter, ones that are easy to manage and directly line up with the strategic vision. Aim for metrics representing progress, steering clear of those that might lead to efforts veering off course.

- Establish a review cycle, ideally every three months, to weigh the current KPIs and goals against the evolving marketplace. This process should include goal-setting, action planning, performance monitoring, and learning from outcomes. Such a structured approach keeps things aligned even as the business landscape shifts.

Measuring decision impact on strategic goals

To make sure our business decisions help us hit our strategic targets, it's crucial to follow a systematic plan. A great way to do this is by setting up ways to keep an eye on and review how things are going. This setup lets a company track the results of its choices and see if they match up with the goals it had in mind or if they're off track. By looking closely at what each decision leads to, companies can spot where their strategies might need a tweak or where some choices didn't quite make the splash they hoped for. Here's an excellent way to tackle this:

- Pin down what success looks like in a way that matches up with your big-picture goals.
- Keep tabs on important indicators of progress regularly.
- Set times to check how healthy actions align with your main aims.

Adding data analysis and key performance metrics into this mix increases its power. Measuring how effectively different decisions push you toward your goals can change the game. This means diving into the data to pick out trends, exceptions, and patterns that shed light on whether your decisions are moving the needle. For a solid approach, consider:

- Zeroing in on data sources filled with insights connected to your goals.
- Using tools to sift through and make sense of this data, especially how it relates to critical outcomes.

- Putting the numbers in context to understand what they mean for your strategy.

Holding regular check-ups is another vital piece of making sure decisions are moving in the right direction. These moments of reflection offer a chance to look back on past choices, thinking about both how they were made and their effects. They also open the door to adjust plans based on new insights, shifting circumstances, and feedback. To do these reviews right, you should:

- Plan frequent sessions that gather everyone playing a part in bringing the strategy to life.
- Look at actual outcomes compared to what was expected and dig into any differences.
- Talk through why these gaps exist and what they mean for staying true to your strategic path.
- Make decisions on how to tweak strategies or change decisions based on what you find.

Moreover, building a culture where everyone feels responsible for ensuring their decisions align with broader objectives is vital. When people own their choices, they're more likely to consider how they affect overall goals. Encouraging this mindset involves:

- Being clear about strategic goals and why it's essential for decisions to reflect them.
- Making sure individuals or teams know which results they're responsible for.

- Celebrating when decisions help meet strategic goals.

- If choices miss the mark, discuss why productively and determine how to do better next time.

Adopting this thorough way of matching decisions with goals highlights the value of continuous monitoring, analyzing, and fine-tuning (USDOT, n.d.). Companies dedicated to these habits stand a much better chance of reaching their strategic markers through informed, purpose-driven choices. It's a business philosophy that makes sure all efforts feed into a bigger picture, helping to navigate the twists and turns of business environments with certainty and intention.

Yet, beyond setting up systems and methods, we're guided by a broader rule: the drive to keep learning and getting better. In our ever-evolving world, being flexible and willing to adjust our strategies and choices is paramount. Weaving a cycle of watchfulness, assessment, and reflection into our strategic plans keeps our approach sharp and in line with our ultimate ambitions.

This way of thinking doesn't just stick rigidly to numbers and metrics. It's about fostering a lively system where feedback loops guide and refine future choices, ensuring they're as close to our strategic aims as possible. It demands an openness to evolution, questioning what we take for granted, and the bravery to shift gears when needed.

Adapting decisions to changing market conditions

Grasping the flow of market trends and understanding your competition is vital when making big decisions in business. In today's ever-changing market, keeping an eye on local and global shifts is crucial. This careful observation allows businesses to anticipate changes and tweak their strategies accordingly, ensuring they're constantly moving toward their primary goals. To stay one step ahead, diving deep into competitor research is essential. This means looking at what products or services competitors offer, how they market themselves, and their business practices to find valuable insights ("5 Secrets to Effective Competitor Research — Greenbook, n.d."). Taking this path helps businesses spot both opportunities and challenges as they come up, leading to more intelligent decisions.

In such a fast-paced world, making quick yet thoughtful decisions is essential for staying in the game. Reacting swiftly to new threats or chances can keep a company competitive. This demands a setup that favors quick decisions without losing sight of the company's overall strategy. To boost this kind of agility, here are a few steps:

- Make sure there's a straightforward way for different departments to talk to each other quickly.

- Get teams from various functions to collaborate on meeting immediate market demands.

- Regularly go over how decisions are made to remove any unnecessary delays.

Adding scenario planning and risk analysis into decision-making equips a business to handle different market situations. This method doesn't try to guess the future but outlines what could happen. By exploring these various outcomes, companies can craft more adaptable strategies. For practical scenario planning and risk analysis, it's helpful in:

- Identify what could majorly change in your industry and imagine several scenarios based on these factors.

- Look at how each scenario could affect your business operations and plans.

- Prepare action plans for the most significant risks identified in your analysis.

Encouraging a mindset where adapting to new decisions is part of the culture means helping teams adjust strategies as markets change. This involves creating an environment where feedback is welcomed, mistakes are seen as learning chances, and flexibility is part of strategic planning. To promote this kind of culture, consider:

- Holding regular sessions to check how well the current market situation fits with your strategy.

- Supporting innovation and trying new things within teams.

- Acknowledging and rewarding those who adapt and take initiative.

As the business world evolves, competitive intelligence powered by AI technologies marks a significant turning point in strategic planning. AI tools are changing how companies gather, analyze, and leverage substantial data sets. These tools can handle unstructured data like social media posts, news articles, and customer reviews, giving a detailed real-time view of the competitive scene ("AI-Powered Competitive Intelligence Transformation Business Strategies in the Digital Age, n.d."). This is a game-changer for companies aiming to stay ahead in today's digital-first era.

Moreover, weaving AI into efforts to gather competitive intelligence boosts decision-making across different areas of a business. With insights into market trends, what competitors are up to, and consumer opinions direct from AI, companies can make well-informed strategic choices closely aligned with their objectives. This level of understanding is vital for making responsive decisions and proactively steering the company's strategic direction with an eye on the future.

Moving from traditional decision-making processes to those enhanced by AI mirrors a broader shift in the business world. As organizations adjust to quick changes, folding technology into strategic planning becomes more critical. This shift doesn't take away from human judgment; instead, it enriches it with deeper insights and forward-looking analytics, allowing for more sophisticated and preemptive decisions.

By embracing these insights, companies can reshape their approach to strategic planning and decision-making. Being well-informed about market trends and competitive dynamics makes it easier to foresee necessary shifts in strategy. Agility in making decisions helps respond to these shifts promptly, and adding scenario planning and risk analysis ensures readiness for different possibilities. Moreover, fostering a proactive stance towards strategy adaptation empowers teams to adjust their approaches in line with changing market conditions. Altogether, these practices provide a solid base for making decisions that are not just reactive but are intentionally aligned with the company's broader aims amidst ongoing market changes.

Ensuring organizational coherence through decisions

Building bridges between different departments and making sure that each person's work meaningfully boosts the company's main goals isn't just a lofty idea—it's a must-have for lasting success. In today's world, where "collaboration" can often seem more of a trendy term than an actual strategy, creating honest cross-departmental communication is critical to aligning choices with the company's goals. But what steps should we take from discussing teamwork to achieving it? Here are a few suggestions:

- Start by encouraging open conversations at every company level so everyone knows how their job contributes to the bigger picture.

- Have regular meetings between different departments to talk about current projects and find opportunities for working together effectively.

- Motivate different teams to establish common objectives that align with the company's overall strategic targets, fostering a sense of unity and purpose.

Shifting focus to how shared values and culture influence decision-making, it's clear that a company's culture plays a massive role in guiding it towards its strategic aims. A culture rich in common values is a beacon for making decisions, directing every choice toward the company's ultimate vision. To promote such a culture:

- Clearly define and communicate the company's core values and vision to ensure everyone understands them.

- Celebrate decisions and behaviors within the company that reflect these values to strengthen the desired culture.

- Offer training and development programs that enhance employees' skills while also emphasizing the company's fundamental values.

When setting up rules and structures for governance, consistency, and transparency are the keywords. Decision-making rules need to be an integral part of the company's daily operations, which involve:

- Creating clear guidelines for decision-making that match the company's strategic aims and making these guidelines known to all staff.

- Formulating a governance framework that enables swift yet well-informed decision-making, including a way to monitor and assess these decisions against the company's goals.

- Ensuring decision-making processes are transparent, boosting trust and responsibility throughout the organization.

Moreover, promoting a culture of learning and feedback is critical for improving decision-making over time. An environment that supports continuous learning allows a company to adjust and grow, keeping its strategies relevant and successful. Ways to create this kind of culture include:

- Setting up venues for sharing insights gained from victories and setbacks, promoting a view of mistakes as growth opportunities.

- Developing methods for collecting and analyzing feedback on the outcomes of decisions, using this information to improve future choices.

- Supporting ongoing professional growth by focusing on better company decision-making skills.

Team alignment is crucial when applying these principles. As the source "Team Alignment: 6 Ways to Create Alignment at Work" highlights, proper alignment goes beyond simple agreement; it means bringing together deeper elements like values, visions, and long-term goals. This reference provides practical tips for creating alignment, such as setting clear organizational objectives, fostering transparent communication, and appreciating team achievements. These tips complement the steps already discussed, emphasizing how cooperation, cultural coherence, consistent decision frameworks, and a robust learning environment contribute to aligning business decisions with strategic objectives.

Key takeaways: Aligning decisions with strategic goals requires a proactive approach to setting objectives, measuring impact, adapting to change, and fostering coherence across the organization. By integrating these principles into decision-making processes, businesses can enhance their strategic alignment and drive sustainable success.

In this chapter, we've explored how making decisions that are in tune with your company's big-picture goals isn't just about ticking boxes. It's about thoughtfully setting aims, keeping an eye on the most critical metrics, and creating a workplace where every choice pushes the team closer to their shared dreams.

This isn't a one-and-done deal. Achieving alignment with strategic goals is an active, ongoing effort. It requires constant reevaluation and flexibility as market trends shift, new technologies emerge, and consumer preferences change. Everyone in the company, from the CEO to the newest employee, plays a crucial role in making sure their actions support the collective goal.

The stakes of sticking to or straying from this course have significant consequences. They affect not just how well the company performs day-to-day but also its ability to stay relevant and competitive over the long haul in a world that never stands still.

References

Augment. (n.d.). *Team Alignment: 6 Ways to Create Alignment at Work*. https://augment.org/blog/team-alignment

Beyond the Balance Sheet. (n.d.). *2.5 Strategic Objectives, Key Performance Indicators, and Targets | Beyond the Balance Sheet*. Retrieved from https://www.ifcbeyondthebalancesheet.org/about-the-toolkit/strategy/strategic-objectives-and-kpis

Biden, A. (2023). *Types of Monitoring and Evaluation. tools4dev*. Retrieved from https://tools4dev.org/blog/types-of-monitoring-and-evaluation/

Gratton, L., & Erickson, T. (2007). *Eight ways to build collaborative teams. Harvard Business Review*. https://hbr.org/2007/11/eight-ways-to-build-collaborative-teams

Greenbook. (n.d.). *5 Secrets to Effective Competitor Research*. Retrieved from https://www.greenbook.org/insights/research-methodologies/5-secrets-to-effective-competitor-research

Harlow, J. (n.d.). *HOW TO DEVELOP KPIS / PERFORMANCE MEASURES. KPI.org*. Retrieved from https://www.kpi.org/kpi-basics/kpi-development/

Harvard Business Review. (2020). *Create KPIs That Reflect Your Strategic Priorities*. https://hbr.org/2020/02/create-kpis-that-reflect-your-strategic-priorities

Harvard Business Review. (2023). *Becoming More Collaborative — When You Like to Be in Control. Harvard Business Review*. Retrieved from https://hbr.org/2023/03/becoming-more-collaborative-when-you-like-to-be-in-control

International Institute for Environment and Development. (n.d.). *Monitoring and evaluation, and impact evaluation methods*. Retrieved from https://www.iied.org/monitoring-evaluation-impact-evaluation-methods

Strategic Consortium of Intelligence Professionals. (n.d.). *AI-Powered Competitive Intelligence Transforming Business Strategies in the Digital Age*. SCIP. https://www.scip.org/news/668613/AI-Powered-Competitive-Intelligence-Transforming-Business-Strategies-in-the-Digital-Age-.htm

U.S. Department of Transportation. (n.d.). *Chapter 7 Monitoring, Evaluation, and Feedback*. Retrieved from https://highways.dot.gov/safety/hsip/shsp/strategic-highway-safety-plan-implementation-process-model/chapter-7-monitoring

Leadership's Role in Decision-Making

In today's fast-paced business world, leadership is the guiding light that helps steer the company through the complex decision-making process. Effective organizations thrive on their ability to make quick and well-informed choices. However, this is easier said than done. The decision-making process is complicated, reflecting the complex nature of human thought. This complexity brings many challenges that can hinder even the most experienced leaders, highlighting the importance of solid leadership in overcoming these obstacles.

A common challenge many companies face is creating an environment where decisions are made effectively, balancing strong leadership with empowering the team. It's crucial to build a culture that welcomes and values different opinions. Unfortunately, it's too easy for teams to become echo chambers, emphasizing the same ideas and neglecting fresh, innovative thoughts. This limits creativity and prevents the team from tapping into a wide range of insights and expertise, highlighting the importance of leadership styles that promote diversity of thought within decision-making teams.

Building Decision-Making Teams for Success

Crafting a top-notch decision-making team is much like an art, focusing on the mix of people involved and the setting they work in. A crucial ingredient for such teams is to welcome diversity within their ranks.

Having a mix of different viewpoints, backgrounds, and skills can significantly boost the decisions made. Imagine a team as a colorful mosaic where each piece, unique in shape and color, comes together to form a stunning image that no single piece could achieve alone. For leaders eager to embrace this variety, here's what to keep in mind:

- Strive to bring in team members from various fields or areas of expertise to broaden understanding.

- Make sure the team reflects a wide range of cultures, backgrounds, and life experiences, enhancing the richness of discussions.

- Try to include individuals at different career stages, merging new perspectives with experienced judgment.

It is equally important to encourage a team dynamic where everyone feels free to contribute their thoughts. This means cultivating an atmosphere that welcomes challenges to the status quo. Leaders can foster such an environment by:

- Organizing regular brainstorming sessions where every suggestion holds equal weight.

- Promoting a culture of constructive commentary, focusing on ideas rather than the individuals presenting them.

- Offering ways for team members to anonymously voice their ideas or concerns, ensuring even the shyest person can speak up.

Achieving a balance between providing clear leadership and offering the freedom for creative thinking requires skill. Team leaders should outline explicit objectives while allowing the team to discover the best paths to these goals. This can involve:

- Defining specific, achievable targets for the team's work.
- Permitting members to organize themselves according to their strengths and interests when tackling tasks or projects.
- Maintaining regular contact to provide support and direction without overstepping into micromanagement.

Building trust and open communication is critical for an efficient decision-making team. Honesty and responsibility ought to be key pillars of how the team functions. Achieving this includes:

- Encouraging members to openly discuss their triumphs and mistakes, fostering a culture focused on learning.
- Holding frequent meetings to keep everyone updated and involved in choosing directions and strategies.
- Creating a respectful feedback environment, with all feedback aimed at furthering the team's collective mission.

Evidence supports the idea that diverse and empowered teams lead to superior decision-making. The research highlighted by the Harvard Business Review (2020) points out the strength of gathering individuals with various outlooks and experiences, stating that this diversity significantly reduces the risks tied to groupthink and biases.

Empowering Employees in Decision Processes

Empowering employees to participate in decision-making is crucial, starting with entrusting them with the autonomy to make decisions. This means thoughtfully assigning responsibilities so people can use their knowledge to the fullest and take responsibility for the results. Here's what effective delegation looks like:

- Understand and align the complexity of decisions with the skills and experiences of your employees.

- Set clear limits on their decision-making power to avoid confusion and overlapping duties.

- Ensure they have the resources and information needed for well-informed decisions.

- Offer regular, constructive feedback to encourage a culture of learning and continual improvement.

By delegating effectively, employees feel more invested in their work and understand their importance in achieving the company's goals. Additionally, it eases the load on management, freeing up time for leaders to plan strategies and innovate.

However, empowering staff goes further than task delegation; it includes nurturing their development through various training programs. Equipping employees with the right tools and knowledge prepares them to tackle complex issues successfully. Organizations can:

- Pinpoint skill shortages and create specific training to address these gaps.

- Motivate attendance at workshops and seminars that support both the company's objectives and the employee's career ambitions.

- Encourage ongoing education by rewarding learning achievements.

- Pair less experienced employees with mentors for valuable insights and guidance.

Investing in employee growth enhances their confidence in making tough decisions and fosters loyalty and personal advancement within the organization.

Creating an environment that supports employees is equally vital. This means developing a space where taking risks is welcomed and failures are seen as learning opportunities. To achieve this:

- Promote transparent communication, making everyone feel respected and listened to.

- Boost innovative thinking by letting employees try out new ideas.

- Share stories of past failures as learning points, minimizing the fear associated with risk-taking.

- Celebrate both the effort and achievements to keep morale high.

Such an atmosphere encourages creative problem-solving and resilience, which are essential for navigating today's complex business world. It also builds trust between staff and management, increasing their readiness to take on new challenges.

Rewarding and recognizing good decision-making reinforces this empowerment culture. Acknowledgment is proof of an individual's contributions to the company's goals. For an impactful recognition program:

- Define clear standards for effective decision-making and keep these goals realistic and transparent.

- Use various appreciation methods, from official awards to informal meeting shout-outs.

- Tailor rewards to suit the recipient's taste or professional goals.

- Give recognition promptly to enhance its significance.

Celebrating successful decisions motivates employees and sets a standard for excellence. This practice creates a healthy competitive spirit, driving innovation.

Employees supported with the proper tools, guidance, and recognition become invaluable to any organization. Their improved decision-making capabilities benefit their personal development and contribute to the company's success. A study in the Harvard Business Review (2023) emphasizes giving employees freedom, linking autonomy with increased innovation, performance, and motivation. This connection addresses the 'decision deficit'—the disparity between the intention to empower and the reality felt by employees. Failing to bridge this gap can result in dissatisfaction and lack of progress.

Cultivating a Culture of Informed Choices

In an era where change is the only constant, making intelligent decisions quickly is more important than ever. This means that organizations need to embrace a way of working where decisions are made based on solid data and thorough analysis. It's not enough to have a lot of data at your fingertips; it's about creating a space where people feel encouraged and supported to dig into this data and use it wisely.

To build an environment that prizes informed decision-making, companies should begin by ensuring information is easily accessible to everyone. This involves removing any barriers that might block the free flow of data and promoting open conversations about what the data shows and what it means for the company. For example, holding regular meetings where teams can share data insights and think together about applying them could be extremely helpful. Also, offering training and resources that help employees understand and analyze data better will enable them to make smarter decisions.

Alongside using data effectively, companies need to encourage their employees to keep learning constantly. The aim here is to keep up with changes in the industry, understand market trends, and stay aware of new technologies that could affect how decisions need to be made. Arranging workshops, online seminars, and other educational events on relevant subjects can support this goal. Moreover, setting up internal forums or discussion circles fosters a culture of knowledge sharing, allowing employees to benefit from each other's experiences and insights.

Creating an atmosphere where experimentation and innovative thinking are valued is just as critical. This mindset promotes creative problem-solving and thinking outside the norm when making decisions. One approach that works well is adopting a 'fail-fast' attitude, encouraging team members to try out new ideas without fear of failure, and understanding that these efforts will lead to valuable lessons—celebrating both successes and mistakes as learning opportunities emphasizes the significance of taking risks in the quest for innovation.

Leaders are essential in illustrating what it means to make informed, strategic decisions. They should set an example, showing how to use data, insights, and goals to guide their choices. When leaders prioritize decisions based on evidence, they send a powerful message throughout the organization, highlighting the importance of making well-informed choices (Harvard Business Review, 2021).

By focusing on these areas—utilizing data effectively, promoting ongoing learning, valuing creativity, and leading by example—companies can forge a strong culture of making informed decisions. This kind of culture doesn't just improve the quality of decisions; it also makes the organization more agile and resilient. It's about laying down a foundation where every team member feels capable and driven to contribute to the company's success with intelligent, well-informed decisions.

So, what steps can you take to move toward this goal? First, make sure there's a system in place for gathering, analyzing, and sharing data efficiently. This may mean investing in better analytics tools or systems that make it easier to access useful data insights.

Next, look for ways to enable continuous learning and professional growth. Whether through structured training programs, mentoring schemes, or collaborative projects, it's important to provide avenues for employees to broaden their horizons and develop new skills.

Then, encourage your teams to innovate and experiment. Think about creating rewards for inventive ideas and ensuring a straightforward process for bringing them to the forefront and giving them a trial run.

Lastly, I'd like you to make the change you want to see. Leaders' commitment to making informed decisions powerfully shapes the organization's culture. Leaders should openly share their thought processes when making decisions, spotlighting evidence and data's role in informing their choices.

Navigating Ethical Considerations in Decision-Making

Every organization faces the crucial task of making decisions that aren't just effective and morally right. It's like walking a tightrope where keeping your balance and moving with precision is critical. This journey starts with laying down solid ethical guidelines and a foundation of values. Think of these guidelines as a compass guiding the organization's decision-making. These principles must match the organization's core values and sit well with society's expectations. For example, if a company prioritizes sustainability, its decisions should always consider environmental ethics.

Creating an environment where ethical issues take center stage means it's important to encourage open talks about ethical quandaries. It's much like airing out a room that's gotten stuffy – it freshens up the entire space. Employees can voice their concerns and exchange ideas on moral responsibilities by setting up a safe zone for these discussions. This openness can lead to better-informed decisions. But how do we make sure these conversations are helpful and result in actual insights? Having some rules of engagement can guide these talks effectively:

- Let team members bring up ethical challenges they encounter.
- Structure the discussions so everyone's viewpoints get a fair hearing.
- Share stories of how past ethical issues were addressed.
- Stress the importance of keeping things confidential and respecting diverse opinions.

Adding training in ethical decision-making forms another critical support beam in this structure. It gives leaders and employees the necessary skills to spot, evaluate, and handle ethical dilemmas properly. This could mean participating in workshops, seminars, or online courses that put a practical spin on ethics within business situations. It's similar to providing navigators with the best maps and compasses so they can steer their ships through dangerous waters safely.

Putting into place ways to monitor and review the ethical impact of decisions helps catch any oversights early and provides chances to adjust the course as needed. This continuous watchfulness keeps the organization's actions aligned with its ethical pledges. Here's what organizations can do to maintain strict ethical oversight:

- Set up an ethics committee to watch over decision-making processes.
- Create a system for reporting unethical actions.

- Keep the ethical guidelines up to date with societal changes and the evolution of organizational values.

- Carry out regular ethics audits to ensure compliance with the set ethical standards.

Mastering the art of ethical decision-making in organizations is challenging yet attainable. It calls for establishing clear ethical benchmarks, encouraging open discussions on ethics, offering specialized training, and maintaining vigilant ethical supervision. By taking these steps, organizations can foster a culture of honesty, steering their decision-making in a direction that benefits everyone involved (University, n.d.).

It's essential to acknowledge that aiming for ethical excellence has obstacles. Organizations exist in changing environments where ethical dilemmas can pop up unexpectedly. Yet, by weaving ethical considerations into their decision-making fabric, organizations can more effectively face these challenges, boosting their reputation and earning trust from employees, customers, and the wider community.

Enhancing Decision-Making Across the Organization

In exploring the critical role leaders have in shaping teams adept at making sound decisions, we've looked into how diversity within these groups is a golden key. It's all about creating an atmosphere where everyone feels welcome and essential, letting their different views shine. This makes the decision-making richer and helps avoid the common traps of uniform thinking and biases.

Moving forward, we discussed various tactics leaders can use to boost decision-making. These ranged from promoting open dialogue to stressing the importance of ethical considerations. The main goal has been to create spaces that value decisions based on solid evidence and encourage ongoing learning. Leaders find themselves in the crucial position of providing clear direction while allowing enough freedom for creative solutions to emerge.

For those looking to improve their decision-making skills within their companies, taking active steps to develop these skills is essential. Such efforts have a wide-reaching impact, fostering a culture that appreciates well-informed, ethical, and diverse insights.

References

HBR. (2020). *7 Strategies for Better Group Decision-Making. Harvard Business Review.* Retrieved from https://hbr.org/2020/09/7-strategies-for-better-group-decision-making

Harvard Business Review. (2021). *Company culture is everyone's responsibility.* https://hbr.org/2021/02/company-culture-is-everyones-responsibility

Harvard Business Review. (2023). *5 Strategies to Empower Employees to Make Decisions. Harvard Business Review.* https://hbr.org/2023/03/5-strategies-to-empower-employees-to-make-decisions

Harvard Business School Online. (2020). *Why Managers Should Involve Their Team in Decision-Making. Business Insights Blog.* https://online.hbs.edu/blog/post/team-decision-making

Harvard Business School Online. (2020). *Why managers should involve their team in decision-making. Business Insights Blog.* Retrieved from https://online.hbs.edu/blog/post/team-decision-making

Harvard Business School Online. (2023). *7 Ways to Improve Your Ethical Decision-Making. Business Insights Blog.* https://online.hbs.edu/blog/post/ethical-decision-making-process

RVC. (2023). *Decisions, decisions: Choosing the right decision-making approach for your organizational culture. Changemakers Blog.* Retrieved from https://rvcseattle.org/2022/11/26/decisions-

decisions-choosing-the-right-decision-making-approach-for-your-organizational-culture/

Santa Clara University. (n.d.). *A Framework for Ethical Decision Making*. Retrieved from https://www.scu.edu/ethics/ethics-resources/a-framework-for-ethical-decision-making/

U.S. Office of Personnel Management. (n.d.). *Effective teams strive for consensus.* Retrieved from https://www.opm.gov/policy-data-oversight/performance-management/teams/effective-teams-strive-for-consensus/

University of California, San Diego. (n.d.). *Ethics Awareness.* Blink. Retrieved from https://blink.ucsd.edu/finance/accountability/ethics-awareness.html

Yates, J. F., & de Oliveira, S. (2016). *Culture and decision making. Organizational Behavior and Human Decision Processes*, 136(106). https://doi.org/10.1016/j.obhdp.2016.05.003

Ye, P., Liu, L., & Tan, J. (2022). *Influence of leadership empowering behavior on employee innovation behavior: The moderating effect of personal development support. Frontiers in Psychology*, 13, 10.3389/fpsyg.2022.1022377. https://doi.org/10.3389/fpsyg.2022.1022377

Continuous Improvement through Decision Analysis

Looking back on our decisions and their outcomes does more than show us what went right or wrong. Think of it as a guiding light that helps us navigate through the fog of uncertainty, leading us toward making smarter decisions ahead. In today's fast-moving world, where every choice might lead to entirely different paths, grasping the significance of our past decisions is essential. Reflecting on these isn't merely looking back—it's a clever personal and professional advancement strategy.

Yet, this crucial step is often missed in the rush to meet immediate objectives and tackle current issues. Many professionals find themselves stuck in a pattern of making the same decisions over and over without stopping to assess if their choices are truly serving them well. This cycle can result in stagnation, where progress stalls not because of insufficient effort but because of not learning from past actions. The real challenge is acknowledging the value of reflection and finding ways to fit it into our hectic lives.

Valuing Post-Decision Analysis

Grasping the importance of evaluating our choices after the fact isn't just about tweaking how we do things or getting better results next time; it's a vital part of building a culture about learning and evolving. When we take the time to look back at the decisions we've made, we discover patterns and insights that are incredibly useful for making smarter decisions in the future. This isn't just about dwelling on the past but using it as a springboard to achieve greater heights.

To get to the bottom of how our decisions play out and to find out where we might need to make some adjustments, it's essential to have an organized way of examining things. Here's a simple plan you could follow to make this kind of reflection a regular part of your or your organization's routine:

- Make it a habit to review your decisions and their outcomes, perhaps after wrapping up a project or at regular times throughout the year.

- Adopt a method to assess how you made the decision and the outcome, comparing what you hoped would happen with what you did.

- Bring in different viewpoints to ensure a thorough evaluation. Different people may see different reasons why something was a success or a failure.

This strategy turns our wins and losses into chances to learn, creating a space where getting better is always in sight and being adaptable is a primary focus.

Equally important in making our after-action reviews more effective is incorporating feedback from everyone involved. By listening to a range of views, we get a more detailed picture of how things turned out. This also means that everyone who had a stake in the decision feels they're part of the conversation, which helps build openness and trust across the board.

Reflecting on our past choices encourages a growth mindset within groups and organizations. It's about shifting from blaming when things don't go as planned to seeing every result as a chance to improve. This change in outlook is crucial for creating an environment where constant enhancement is part of how things are done.

And when it comes to making sure we're learning as much as we can from these reflections, involving everyone's feedback is critical. To do this effectively, try the following:

- Pin down who needs to weigh in for each decision and set up easy ways for them to share their thoughts.

- Promote open and constructive feedback by keeping it anonymous or confidential.

- listen to what people are saying and look for common threads that might need more attention.

- Let everyone know how their suggestions have led to changes or new approaches.

Getting everyone involved not only improves the process of reviewing decisions but also leads to a stronger, more inclusive way of deciding things moving forward. This push for inclusiveness ensures that a broad set of experiences and insights shape smarter, informed choices.

Regularly checking in on our past decisions with these methods improves our understanding of what worked and what didn't. Learning from this ensures we don't keep making the same mistakes and helps us repeat our successes. This cycle of doing, reflecting, learning, and then acting again lies at the heart of developing decision-making practices that are effective, adaptable, and meet the demands of today's challenges.

As Beccue et al. (n.d.) pointed out, it's also essential to recognize that decision analysis, which is part of applied mathematics, provides deep insights into how to better our decision-making. By focusing on making good moves regardless of how things turn out, stressing the need to declare decisions, leading with our values, identifying all possible options, and using trustworthy information, individuals and organizations can significantly boost how they make decisions. This approach underlines the importance of being clear-headed and intentional, vital for tackling complex issues and achieving our goals.

Iterative Decision-Making Benefits

Adopting a step-by-step approach to making decisions is like unlocking a new level of understanding in our ever-changing world. It's all about realizing that our choices might need a little tweaking as new facts come to light or as situations evolve. This idea is essential today because quickly adapting without losing sight of our long-term goals is crucial.

Starting this method is about something other than constantly changing directions on a whim. What it involves is a planned way to remain flexible. By checking in regularly on our choices, people and businesses can keep up with the pace without straying from their primary objectives. Here's how you can make this happen:

- Set a timetable for revisiting your decisions. Depending on how quickly things change around you, this could be every quarter, month, or even week.

- Develop a method for weighing new information as it arrives, figuring out how it affects your current plans.

- Promote a culture where everyone's input is valued, ensuring those on the frontline can help fine-tune decisions.

As we revisit our decisions over time, it's fantastic to see how this cycle can polish and sharpen our decisions. By taking another look at our choices, we allow ourselves to refine them, taking into account new insights and shifts in the environment. To get better at this, here's what you can do:

- Keep track of how things pan out after deciding so you have a reference point for improvements.

- Foster honest conversations about what's working and what isn't, viewing feedback as a chance for growth.

- Employ data analysis to uncover trends and insights that might not be immediately clear, laying a solid foundation for adjustments.

On the other hand, considering decisions as stepping stones rather than isolated choices helps us see them as part of a bigger picture, linking each choice more closely to our overall strategy. This mindset is essential for staying aligned with strategic goals while navigating an unpredictable world.

Furthermore, encouraging a spirit of trial and error within the decision-making realm naturally stems from this iterative stance. Viewing decisions as ongoing paths to improvement lessens the fear of messing up and boosts a readiness to try new things. Cultivating such an environment doesn't just magically happen; it takes a concerted effort to celebrate the small victories and learn from any hiccups without pointing fingers. This creates a vibrant space where innovative ideas are welcomed and cherished.

The continuous process improvement (CPI) and Lean/Six Sigma (LSS) methodologies introduced by the Defense Acquisition University showcase the strength of gradual enhancements in boosting operational performance. These practices embody the spirit of iterative decision-making through a systematic and rigorous approach aimed at minimizing waste, managing variability, and relentlessly pursuing small and significant advancements. Their adoption by the Department of Defense leaders highlights the substantial advantages they offer in terms of efficiency and effectiveness, perfectly illustrating the core benefits of this decision-making style.

Feedback Loops for Decision Refinement

Creating an environment where feedback isn't just taken but also actively sought and used to make better decisions marks a big step forward for more open and effective operations in businesses or public administrations. At the heart of this shift are feedback loops, which play a vital role by enabling ongoing refinement and enhancement. They act as a system for using insights from different viewpoints to shape decisions, ensuring that these decisions are grounded in real-life experiences and not just theoretical knowledge.

Feedback loops open up communication lines, analyzing past actions and decisions not to place blame but to learn and grow from them. They operate on the basic yet impactful idea that every choice and action creates ripples within an organization or community, whose impacts must be observed, reviewed, and integrated into the system. This loop allows for immediate tweaks and changes, which is crucial in today's fast-moving world, where failing to evolve can lead to falling behind. For example, if a new product doesn't hit its targets, quick feedback can lead to prompt actions that might save the product's success and customer satisfaction. This ability to react and adapt quickly is at the heart of continuous improvement, helping prevent minor issues from becoming major problems.

Moreover, feedback loops encourage teamwork and cooperation among all involved parties. This collaboration breaks down barriers, ensuring every part of an organization or community works together towards common goals and understands each other. This unity creates a more synchronized environment where insights from one area can benefit others, leading to more robust and more comprehensive decision-making.

Adopting these feedback systems also shows a dedication to openness and honesty. When everyone knows their thoughts and opinions are valued and considered, it builds trust and establishes a culture of responsibility. More than just improving decision-making, this openness strengthens the whole organization or societal structure, making it more flexible and resilient.

To put continuous feedback into practice effectively, having some guidelines can be helpful, especially for organizations just starting this shift. Steps to start could include running short, regular surveys to check how satisfied people are and what they think about recent decisions or changes; creating easy-to-use channels for sharing feedback anytime; looking at feedback data as it comes to spot trends, surprises, and chances for getting better; and allowing teams to make needed changes swiftly, without getting slowed down by too much red tape.

These actions provide a foundation for fostering a mindset focused on feedback throughout an organization or community's daily operations.

Research also supports the power of feedback loops to improve decision-making processes. In their study, Markey, Reichheld, and Dullweber (2009) highlight how companies that use Net Promoter Scores (NPS) to gather feedback quickly act on what they learn from their customers, leading to better service and keeping customers coming back. This shows the clear advantages of connecting feedback directly with action, positively impacting satisfaction levels and how well operations run.

Such practical examples show that feedback loops aren't just theoretical ideas; they're valuable tools for making ongoing improvements. They demonstrate the 'act, assess, adjust' cycle that can significantly enhance the quality of decisions and the overall well-being of organizations.

Advocating for Data-Driven Decision Analysis

Embracing a data-driven approach in decision-making is advantageous; it's necessary for crafting well-informed strategies that resonate with an organization's goals and ambitions. This technique emphasizes making decisions grounded on concrete evidence, moving away from solely depending on gut feelings or previous experiences. It involves smartly using statistical information, understanding patterns, and identifying trends to direct decision-making. By doing so, solid, credible evidence supports every strategic step taken.

To shift towards a data-oriented perspective in decision-making, here are a few steps you can follow:

- Start by gathering quality, relevant data. This is crucial because the quality of your decisions will directly depend on the quality of your data.

- Put money into acquiring data analytics tools. These instruments are vital in uncovering trends and patterns that might go unnoticed.

- Make sure your team understands the value of these tools and knows how to use them. Accurate data reading is vital.

- Keep revisiting and tweaking your decision-making strategy with fresh data. Adopting this repeating cycle makes sure your plans stay up-to-date and effective.

Opting for data-driven decision analysis brings an impartial viewpoint to evaluating our options, offering a level of objectivity that personal judgment alone cannot provide. It improves the precision and trustworthiness of our decisions, basing them on tangible, actionable insights instead of guesswork. This shift toward making evidence-based decisions reduces risks and helps avoid costly mistakes (HBS Online, 2019).

Moreover, bringing data into the equation of decision analysis doesn't just help spot new trends but also equips organizations to act swiftly. This quickness is crucial in today's rapidly changing business world, where staying ahead can be the difference between leading the market and struggling to keep up.

However, adopting a culture focused on data isn't without its challenges. Organizations face hurdles such as managing data collection, storage, and analysis complexities, protecting against data breaches, and complying with laws. There's also the challenge of fostering an employee mindset that welcomes data-centric decision-making despite potential resistance or doubts about this seemingly impersonal decision-making method.

Despite these obstacles, switching to a data-focused mindset is valuable. Beyond improving decision accuracy, it cultivates an environment of ongoing enhancement. Organizations can develop more dynamically through consistent analysis of outcomes and fine-tuning strategies over time. This ongoing cycle of learning and adapting serves as a robust foundation for innovation and growth.

At the core, prioritizing data-driven methods enables organizations to face uncertainties with more assurance. It allows leaders to make choices informed by current conditions and foresighted toward future scenarios. From my perspective, valuing hard facts and detailed analysis, adopting data-driven decision-making is not just a smart move but a duty towards those we aim to serve—our customers, stakeholders, or communities.

Harnessing Insights for Superior Decision-Making

In this chapter, we've explored how constantly seeking improvement by looking back at our previous decisions and their results can lead us to growth. Remembering our initial discussions, we discussed the importance of learning from what we've done before as a critical step toward making more intelligent choices. Right now, we're advocating for an environment where feedback is valued, analyses are based on data, and decision-making is constantly evolving. These elements are crucial for anyone aiming to get better at making decisions.

This conversation should strike a chord with professionals from all backgrounds who recognize how polishing their decision-making skills can significantly affect their achievements and the success of their organizations. Realizing the downsides of sticking to old decision-making habits makes it clear how important it is to stay competitive, innovative, and resilient, significantly when the world is constantly changing.

References

DASCA. (n.d.). *How Does Data-Driven Decision Making Improve Business Outcomes?* Retrieved from https://www.dasca.org/world-of-data-science/article/how-does-data-driven-decision-making-improve-business-outcomes

Defense Acquisition University. (n.d.). *Continuous process improvement (CPI) and Lean/Six Sigma (LSS)*. Retrieved from https://www.dau.edu/acquipedia-article/continuous-process-improvement-cpi-and-lean/six-sigma-lss

Economics Web Institute. (n.d.). *The positive and negative feedback mechanisms and loops were explained. Software and data*. Economics Web Institute. Retrieved from http://www.economicswebinstitute.org/glossary/feedback.htm

Feedback Labs. (2016). *3TT: Why Feedback is crucial for Inclusive Decision Making*. Retrieved from https://feedbacklabs.org/blog/2016/10/27/feedback-and-inclusive-decision-making/

HBS Online. (2019). *The Advantages of Data-Driven Decision-Making. Business Insights Blog*. Retrieved from https://online.hbs.edu/blog/post/data-driven-decision-making

Hanna, R. (2009). *Closing the customer feedback loop. Harvard Business Review*. Retrieved from https://hbr.org/2009/12/closing-the-customer-feedback-loop

IES (n.d.). *Data-driven decision-making in education: How REL work makes a difference*. Retrieved from https://ies.ed.gov/blogs/ncee/post/data-driven-decision-making-in-education-how-rel-work-makes-a-difference

Manlapig, E., & Beccue, P. (Year of Publication). *What I Learned from Pokémon and Other Games. Title of the Journal*. DOI or URL.

National Implementation Research Network. Practicing Implementation: PDSA Cycles: Improvement and Implementation. Retrieved from https://nirn.fpg.unc.edu/practicing-implementation/pdsa-cycles-improvement-and-implementation

O'Donnell, B., & Gupta, V. (2023). *Continuous quality improvement. StatPearls [Internet]*. Retrieved from https://www.ncbi.nlm.nih.gov/books/NBK559239/

Tulane University School of Public Health. (2022). *Data-Driven Decision-Making for Health Administrators*. School of Public Health. Retrieved from https://publichealth.tulane.edu/blog/data-driven-decision-making/

USAID Learning Lab. (2024). *Data-Driven Decision Making: The Missing Piece in Development Projects*. Retrieved from https://usaidlearninglab.org/community/blog/data-driven-decision-making-missing-piece-development-projects

Decision-Making in Uncertain Environments

Navigating the unpredictable waves of today's business world is becoming increasingly important. The skill to make well-thought-out decisions, even in constantly changing situations and full of surprises, is crucial for any company wishing to survive and grow. Nowadays, businesses are hit from all sides with new challenges: rapid technological growth, fluctuating markets, and shifts in the global economy. These factors create uncertainty, making it challenging for old-school decision-making methods to keep up.

The real challenge lies in facing uncertainty and dealing with its complexity and the speed at which changes happen. Old ways of planning and forecasting need to be quicker and more flexible to handle today's fast-paced world. This makes it dangerously easy to make decisions that have not been thought through properly. Facing such a quicksand of change, companies often find themselves stuck: too scared to move because they might sink, yet aware that standing still could mean missing out. Finding the right balance between taking intelligent risks and protecting your business's primary goals becomes tricky but essential.

This part of our discussion focuses on strategies that help improve how decisions are made during such uncertain times. It emphasizes how crucial it is for businesses to be adaptable, to foster a culture where learning and evolving are encouraged, and to outline steps for staying flexible and robust. By embracing continuous learning and planning for different future scenarios, businesses can lay down a solid groundwork that helps them move quickly and think creatively when needed. Moreover, by understanding what levels of risk are acceptable, companies can steer through stormy weather without getting lost. Together, these approaches pave the way forward, enabling businesses to withstand unpredictability and use it as a stepping stone toward new opportunities.

Adaptive Decision-Making: Thriving in Volatility

Making smart decisions in the ever-changing world of business is crucial for success. It's not enough to decide on a path forward; companies must be ready to adjust those decisions as new information comes in and circumstances change. This flexible approach to decision-making acknowledges that change is the only guarantee in business. The companies that stand out are the ones that can quickly shift their direction based on new insights or changes in the market.

Being flexible and agile is critical. These qualities allow companies to grab new opportunities that might pass others by and avoid potential problems before they become more significant. But what does it take to make a company truly flexible and agile? It starts with creating a workplace culture that chooses flexibility over being stuck in its ways. It's about encouraging everyone to think outside the box and welcome change openly. This change in thinking is vital for moving swiftly and effectively, mainly when the market does something unexpected.

Additionally, committing never to stop learning is a secret weapon for thriving in uncertain markets. A company that keeps learning constantly grows, viewing every result—good or bad—as a chance to improve. This dedication to continually adapting helps companies stay relevant and ready to face whatever challenges come their way.

While we've talked about the importance of adapting, actually putting this into practice involves preparing for different scenarios that could happen in the future. This means imagining various situations that could affect your business—not just the things you think will happen but also the less likely, yet still possible, challenges. Then, put your company to the test to see how it would hold up under those scenarios. This preparation helps pinpoint where your company is strong and where it might need to beef up its defenses.

So, how can you get started with this kind of planning? Here's a plan of action:

- First, figure out what significant factors might influence your business down the line. These could be economic shifts, technological breakthroughs, or changes in what customers want.

- Next, imagine several different futures that could unfold from these factors, both the good and the not-so-good.

- For each possible future, think about what strategies you could use, especially those that keep your business agile and adaptable.

- Then, do some stress tests to see how your business would fare in each scenario. Look for strengths and weaknesses.

- Lastly, let what you learn from this process guide your long-term planning. Make sure your strategy is solid enough to handle a variety of what-ifs.

Adopting this structured approach improves decision—making under uncertainty and fosters a culture of adaptability within your team. Being ready for various outcomes lets businesses face unpredictable times more confidently, making quick adjustments to tackle challenges and seize new chances as they appear.

The benefit of being this adaptable really can't be underestimated. In a time when the only sure thing is constant change, being able to pivot and grow is an invaluable asset. Traditional ways of doing things, which rely on predictability, don't cut it anymore. Today's global market moves fast, demanding a fresh strategy that sees uncertainty as an opportunity rather than a barrier.

Indeed, flexibility, agility, and preparedness are essential traits for any company wanting to survive and flourish amid uncertainty. These characteristics ensure businesses can react promptly to surprises, learn from what happens, and keep evolving. By embracing change instead of fearing it, companies set themselves up for enduring success in a constantly changing world.

Risk Tolerance in Uncertain Times: Navigating Through Turbulence

Grasping the significance of how much risk one can tolerate when making decisions amid uncertainties is critical for businesses that aim to prosper in unpredictable markets. At the heart of it, it's not about avoiding risks altogether but recognizing, evaluating, and deciding what level of risk is acceptable. This strategy enables companies to make choices that strive for success while being aware of possible setbacks.

To handle risk tolerance efficiently, companies need to start with a thorough evaluation of potential risks. This step involves pinpointing internal and external factors that might disrupt business goals or operations. After identifying these threats, assessing their likely impact helps sort them by their probability and the extent of their possible effects. Companies must set clear boundaries on what they consider an acceptable risk. Achieving this includes:

- Creating a structured procedure for spotting and evaluating risks.
- Applying methods and tools like SWOT or PESTLE analysis to scrutinize potential dangers methodically.
- Formulating a risk matrix to sort risks by severity and likelihood, thus focusing on the most critical ones.

Once the phase of identification and evaluation is over, it becomes critical to understand the balance between risk and reward. Every uncertain decision entails comparing the potential advantages with the risks involved. Companies should fine-tune their risk tolerance to match their strategic goals and the current market scenario. Making effective decisions requires a harmonious perspective that accounts for immediate benefits and long-term viability. Strategies to maintain this equilibrium include:

- Defining explicit criteria to compare potential profits with the accompanying risks.

- Promoting open dialogues among the leadership to discuss various options and their implications.

- Using data analytics to predict outcomes and evaluate the balance between strategies' risks and rewards.

Building a culture within the organization that is aware of risks significantly aids in making wise decisions. In such a culture, everyone from top to bottom realizes the importance of managing risks and is motivated to spot and minimize them actively. This doesn't necessarily mean imposing more rules but rather integrating risk awareness into daily tasks and choices. Steps to cultivate this mindset involve:

- Offering ongoing training on the fundamentals of risk management.

- Encouraging transparent and honest conversations about uncertainties and risks.

- Appreciating and rewarding actions that contribute to managing risks effectively.

In response to ever-changing circumstances, businesses must continuously revisit and adjust their approach to risk tolerance. Due to fluctuating market dynamics and shifts in organizational capabilities, yesterday's risk levels may not fit today's needs. Remaining competitive requires agility in reassessing risk thresholds and modifying strategies as needed. This process includes:

- Regularly updating statements on risk appetite and tolerance to mirror present conditions.

- Weaving risk management into strategic planning and daily operations for quick adaptations.

- Keep an eye on external and internal changes that could influence risk levels and proactively adjust to maintain alignment with risk tolerance.

Understanding the delicate interplay between risk and reward, determining suitable risk thresholds, nurturing a risk-conscious organizational ethos, and staying adaptable are central to decision-making in uncertain situations. It's all about informed actions, where decisions are based on a deep understanding of the risks involved and their alignment with the company's broader objectives. As the Institute of Risk Management points out, without specific, measurable tolerances, any risk cycle and framework might as well be non-existent. This underscores the necessity of having a detailed plan for risk appetite and tolerance as a fundamental element of risk management in an enterprise.

The Value of Flexibility: Adapting Strategies to Win

In today's ever-changing business world, adapting your decision-making is critical to thriving in unpredictable times. The secret sauce? Flexibility. It helps businesses stay ahead of the curve, grow, and survive over the long haul. Let's dive into how being agile with your strategies can strengthen your organization in the face of uncertainty.

Flexibility in decision-making allows businesses to tackle unexpected challenges head-on quickly. In our fast-moving world, where new opportunities and threats pop up out of nowhere, pivoting swiftly is invaluable. However, developing this agility starts with building a culture that embraces change and innovation. Encourage everyone in your company to think outside the box and generate fresh ideas, highlighting your value of quick and creative thinking.

Here are some practical steps to nurture this environment:

- Make it a habit to ask for feedback from employees at all levels about ways to improve or new strategies to consider.

- Create teams from different departments to work on projects together. This brings varied perspectives and quicker brainstorming of ideas.

- Set up a system to quickly assess how well new methods are working, learning from both successes and failures.

Another tool to boost flexibility is to plan for different future scenarios, even those that seem far-fetched. By thinking ahead about possible developments and their impacts on your business, you're better prepared for whatever comes your way.

Try these tips to get ahead:

- Pinpoint the main external factors, like new technologies or laws, that could significantly affect your company.

- Imagine various future scenarios based on these factors and explore their potential impacts on your business goals and day-to-day operations.

- Prepare action plans for the most critical scenarios, mapping out what steps should be taken should early signs of these situations appear.

Cultivating a spirit of experimentation and seeing mistakes as learning opportunities is crucial for adaptability. This means shaking off the old ways that punish failure and rewarding risks and innovation, even when they don't pan out as expected.

Here's how to foster this mindset:

- Dedicate resources for trying out new ideas outside your main business activities.

- Applaud both the breakthroughs and the noble attempts that didn't quite succeed, focusing on what can be learned from each.

- Seek inspiration by partnering with startups, academic institutions, or other organizations to inject new ideas and technologies into your company.

It's vital to have solid feedback channels and performance indicators in place to keep improving your decision-making process. Being alert to shifts in the market requires knowing what's working and what isn't. This involves collecting and analyzing data on various fronts and applying those insights to tweak and enhance your strategies.

Effective ways to do this include:

- Using dashboards that show real-time stats on crucial aspects of your business, giving you a clearer view of how things are going operationally and strategically.

- Meet regularly with team leaders to review these metrics, spot trends, and pinpoint areas for tweaks or full-on changes.

- Valuing feedback from your employees, customers, and partners, letting their insights guide strategic decisions.

A telling example of the need for adaptability is seen in how businesses navigated the COVID-19 pandemic. Those that managed to flourish were quick on their feet—switching to remote teams, altering their product lines to meet new demands, or moving sales online. Their success stemmed not from predicting the pandemic but from their readiness to try new approaches and adjust rapidly amid total uncertainty (author1 et al., 2011).

Agility and Resilience: Overcoming Unpredictability

In today's world, businesses face a constant barrage of new challenges that can change the game overnight. Being able to pivot and handle these surprises quickly has become essential. Agility is critical—it helps companies recover swiftly, lessen setbacks, and sometimes even discover hidden gems amidst troubles. This agility relies on being one step ahead, always ready for what might come next. Instead of just reacting to problems, successful businesses anticipate them and have plans ready to go. They adopt an approach that's about defending against threats and actively shaping their future.

To stay ahead of the curve, here are some practical steps businesses can take:

- Keep an eye on the environment outside the business to spot dangers and opportunities early on.

- Shape your business model adaptable, making it easy to switch directions.

- Promote a culture where trying new things is encouraged and valued.

Having a team that works together well across all areas of the business is crucial for this kind of swift adaptation. When teams operate in isolation, sharing vital information takes longer, slowing decision-making. But, when everyone works as part of a larger team, information and ideas flow freely. This allows for quick, effective decisions, even in tough times. By working together, the whole organization can tackle issues more effectively, drawing on various viewpoints for more robust solutions.

To boost teamwork, businesses can:

- Hold regular meetings with staff from different parts of the company to talk about big-picture challenges and share insights.

- Use technology that helps everyone communicate and collaborate easily, regardless of where they are.

- Set up a clear plan for making decisions quickly in emergencies, making sure everyone who needs to be involved is.

Technology and the intelligent use of data are also critical for businesses wanting to stay resilient in the face of uncertainty. Advanced analytics allows companies to predict upcoming trends, see potential risks, and make smarter decisions faster. Analyzing data in real-time can uncover issues early on, letting businesses address them before they become more significant problems. Plus, technology can streamline processes and increase efficiency, giving people more time to think strategically and creatively about how to solve problems.

For those wanting to leverage technology and data, here's what to consider:

- Put money into tools that predict market trends and customer behavior.

- Embrace cloud computing to make your operations more flexible and scalable.

- Make sure your cybersecurity is solid and current to fend off digital threats.

Developing a culture within your organization that prioritizes resilience is the most all-encompassing way to navigate unpredictability. A workplace that values quick thinking, innovation, and decisive action can turn obstacles into stepping stones. Such a culture motivates everyone to contribute ideas and embrace changes positively. However, building this kind of environment takes time. It requires consistent leadership and policies that support adaptability, learning, and growth.

Ways to nurture a resilient culture include:

- Leaders should exemplify resilience and flexibility, inspiring others to do the same.

- Support taking risks and learning from mistakes, creating a space where innovation can flourish.

- Offer training focusing on developing the workforce's adaptive leadership and problem-solving skills.

These strategies—being proactive, encouraging teamwork, integrating technology, and fostering a resilient culture—are vital for staying agile and responding effectively to uncertainty. These methods prepare companies to weather storms and help them seize new opportunities during times of change. A Harvard Business Review article from 2020 pointed out how the COVID-19 pandemic made many leaders painfully aware of how fragile their systems were and highlighted the urgent need to rebuild with greater resilience in mind. This shows that resilience isn't just about defense; it's a strategic advantage that lets organizations thrive under new conditions.

Critical Strategies for Decision-Making in Uncertain Environments

In this section, we delve into effective tactics for making well-informed choices amidst the often unpredictable nature of today's business world. We've discussed the value of fostering an environment that prioritizes adaptability and nimbleness alongside recognizing and managing one's capacity for risk. A key takeaway is the importance of quickly adjusting - reminiscent of how a tree bends in a storm without breaking. Similarly, companies must be capable of navigating through changes while staying grounded.

Moving on, both professionals and leaders must acknowledge that the realm of decision-making is continuously changing. The insights provided are not only for immediate application but also for the future. The path might seem intimidating for those charting their course through these rough seas, but it's filled with potential for development, creativity, and achievement.

Adopting or overlooking these strategies affects broader market behavior and overall economic vitality beyond the confines of any single organization. By welcoming change, companies stand to endure, revolutionize their sectors, and establish new benchmarks for exceptional performance.

References

Boston Consulting Group. (2011). *Adaptability: The new competitive advantage. Harvard Business Review.* Retrieved from
https://hbr.org/2011/07/adaptability-the-new-competitive-advantage

Boston Consulting Group. (2011). *Adaptability: The new competitive advantage. Harvard Business Review.*
https://hbr.org/2011/07/adaptability-the-new-competitive-advantage

Gallup, Inc. (2021, June 23). *Top CHROs believe 'flexibility within a framework' is the future of work. Workplace.*
https://www.gallup.com/workplace/351029/top-chros-believe-flexibility-within-framework-future-work.aspx

Harvard Business Review. (2020). *A guide to building a more resilient business.* Retrieved from https://hbr.org/2020/07/a-guide-to-building-a-more-resilient-business

Harvard Business Review. (2022). *In Uncertain Times, the Best Strategy Is Adaptability.* Retrieved from https://hbr.org/2022/08/in-uncertain-times-the-best-strategy-is-adaptability

Harvard Business Review. (2022). *Make resilience your company's strategic advantage. Harvard Business Review.* Retrieved from https://hbr.org/2022/03/make-resilience-your-companys-strategic-advantage

ISACA. (2022). *Risk appetite vs. risk tolerance: What is the difference?* ISACA Now Blog. Retrieved from https://www.isaca.org/resources/news-and-trends/isaca-now-blog/2022/risk-appetite-vs-risk-tolerance-what-is-the-difference

McKee, D. O., Varadarajan, P. R., & Pride, W. M. (1989). *Strategic adaptability and firm performance: A market-contingent perspective. Journal of Marketing*, 53(3), 21-35.
https://www.jstor.org/stable/1251340

Settembre-Blundo, D., González-Sánchez, R., Medina-Salgado, S., & García-Muiña, F. E. (2021). *Flexibility and resilience in corporate decision making: A new sustainability-based risk management system in uncertain times. Global Journal of Flexible Systems Management*, 22(Suppl 2), 107. https://doi.org/10.1007/s40171-021-00277-7

The Institute of Risk Management. (n.d.). *Risk appetite and tolerance.* https://www.theirm.org/what-we-say/thought-leadership/risk-appetite-and-tolerance/

Implementing Decision-Making Best Practices

Making decisions is critical to success and keeping a company firm in the fast-paced business world. As companies move through a constantly changing world, thanks to new technology and evolving customer needs, making smart decisions quickly is more important than ever. It's crucial to have decision-making tools designed to make significant strategic choices and ensure these choices match the company's main goals and values. A toolkit with different tools and methods helps organize the way decisions are made, ensuring every decision allows the company to move forward.

Creating and using a good decision-making process can be challenging, though. With a clear plan, companies might avoid making rushed decisions that don't fit their overall strategy, harming the company's culture of trust and integrity. Finding the right tools and ensuring they fit the business's unique needs can be tricky. Plus, if a company doesn't encourage everyone to get involved and share openly, even the best decision-making plans won't reach their full potential, leaving great ideas and insights on the table.

Building a Decision-Making Toolkit

When making decisions in the business world, it is crucial to take time to understand the complex nature of the environment. Having a clear plan that ties back to what the company strives for and values is essential. This plan should be flexible but serve as a guide to making choices that comply with the company's aims and principles. By making decisions systematically, businesses empower their teams to opt for paths that strengthen their shared vision and maintain fundamental values, promoting a workplace culture of consistency and integrity.

Incorporating various tools and templates into this decision-making process is incredibly helpful. These can include anything from matrices and models that help weigh options to checklists and diagrams that map out steps. The main goal is to pick or create resources that meet your business's unique needs and address specific hurdles you might face. Having these resources makes the decision-making process smoother and increases its effectiveness by ensuring thorough evaluation and minimizing the chance of missing something important.

Recognizing that decisions must be tailored because every situation is different is critical, especially since the business world is never static. Fine-tuning might mean adjusting how much weight specific outcomes have in your model or changing a diagram to show better who needs to approve what. To keep your decision-making toolbox relevant, you could:

1. Identify factors that most affect decision results specific to your business.
2. Set up rules for tweaking the tools based on these factors.
3. Collect examples showing past adjustments.
4. Teach your team how to adapt these tools effectively.

Showing these tools at work through real-life scenarios is an effective way to demonstrate their value. It's one thing to know about a tool theoretically; seeing it in action offers a practical perspective. Real-life success stories make the methods more understandable and relatable, showcasing advantages like clearer understanding, quicker decision-making, and alignment with company goals.

Promoting the creation of a decision-making toolkit that caters specifically to your business's needs emphasizes the idea that while there are general best practices, tailoring approaches to suit an organization's unique identity is crucial. A customized toolkit considers a company's distinct challenges, culture, and strategic direction, ensuring that decisions are not just timely but also closely aligned with what the organization truly represents. Building such a toolkit requires reviewing what worked and didn't and refining tools and techniques with ongoing input and analysis.

At its core, developing a toolkit filled with structured plans, adaptable resources, and practical examples supports a strategic mindset for tackling business decisions. It bridges the gap between theory and the daily realities organizations face. Following guidelines, like those suggested by (Keys to Making Smart Business Decisions | USC Online Communication Degree, n.d.), including setting clear, measurable, agreed-upon, relevant, and time-bound objectives, lays a strong foundation. This comprehensive strategy allows companies to make well-informed decisions, steering them toward their goals and nurturing a culture of strategic thought and continuous growth. Ultimately, this approach helps build resilience and flexibility within an organization, which are vital qualities in today's ever-changing business environment.

Cultivating a Decision-Forward Organizational Culture

Integrating decision-making into an organization's culture is like guiding a ship toward its destination. It involves more than having directions; it demands a team that talks openly, understands the path forward, and collaborates effortlessly toward their goal. Using this metaphor highlights the importance of open communication in making informed decisions. When everyone in the organization is notified, understands why decisions are made, and feel their input is valued, a foundation of trust is laid. This forms the basis for a culture where transparency and accountability flourish.

Incorporating these decision-making processes into everyday business activities and planning reveals that such practices should be more comprehensive than those of top management. Spreading these responsibilities across every level nurtures a feeling of ownership and responsibility among workers. This method makes the decision-making process inclusive and benefits from the wide range of perspectives and insights present throughout the company. It's about acknowledging that anyone, regardless of their role or title, can offer valuable ideas and critical thinking.

Encouraging collaborative decision-making efforts among all involved parties underlines the need for collective action to navigate the organization successfully. Collaboration here involves everyone - including employees, customers, and suppliers. This approach recognizes how interconnected an organization's environment is and creates a culture where everyone's contributions make a more significant impact. Such teamwork is vital in today's fast-moving and interconnected global scene, where challenges have become too complicated for isolated attempts.

It is equally crucial to highlight the role of ongoing learning in embedding decision-making as a core value within the organization. The world around us changes continuously—new technologies arise, market conditions evolve, and successful strategies may become obsolete overnight. Organizations ensure they stay relevant and competitive by fostering a culture that values learning and adaptability. Ongoing learning drives innovation, increases employee engagement, and improves decision-making outcomes.

Steps to achieve this include initiating platforms for consistent open dialogue, like town hall meetings or feedback sessions, to ensure every voice is heard. Creating cross-functional teams for strategic discussions brings together diverse viewpoints and expertise, breaking down barriers within the company. Additionally, setting up frameworks for joint decision-making through shared digital spaces where stakeholders can offer ideas and feedback is essential. Lastly, developing and supporting opportunities for learning via workshops, seminars, and online courses promotes personal and professional development.

Moving towards a culture that emphasizes efficient and effective decision-making requires dedication, leadership, and foresight. Yet, the benefits — a more responsive, innovative, and cohesive organization — are significant. Research from the Harvard Business Review (2020) points out that the main hurdles in creating a data-driven culture, which directly impacts decision-making, are cultural rather than technical. This highlights the importance of focusing on the artistic aspects to improve organizational decision-making.

To effectively link theory with practice, the focus must be on practical steps to foster the desired cultural shifts. Each recommendation provided is a building block toward achieving a culture where informed and cooperative decisions are the norm. In doing so, organizations are positioning themselves for success and contributing to a broader change in how businesses operate and innovate today.

Strategies for Effective Decision Implementation

In this section of our discussion, we've taken a deep dive into how businesses can improve decisions. We've talked about building tools specific to each company and creating a culture that values good decision-making. We started by highlighting the importance of companies making sure their decision-making aligns with what they stand for and their primary goals. This means choosing strategies carefully to fit the unique situation of each business.

As we circle back to where we began, it's clear that having various tools and a culture that encourages learning and values everyone's input is crucial. Through this, businesses aren't just deciding on things; they are on a collective journey to reach their goals, built on trust, openness, and shared wisdom.

We've reached a critical point in the conversation where taking these steps is more than just a good idea—it's essential. In today's fast-changing business world, companies that tweak their decision-making to be more open, flexible, and aligned with their main objectives will have an edge over the competition.

This whole examination is aimed at anyone looking to excel in making decisions. It indicates that putting these methods into practice could profoundly affect not just individual businesses but the entire industry, leading toward a more strategic and unified future.

References

Clark, E. C., Burnett, T., Blair, R., Traynor, R. L., Hagerman, L., & Dobbins, M. (2024). *Strategies to implement evidence-informed decision making at the organizational level: a rapid systematic review. BMC Health Services Research*, 24(10). https://doi.org/10.1186/s12913-024-10841-3

Harvard Business Review. (2020). *10 Steps to Creating a Data-Driven Culture*. Retrieved from https://hbr.org/2020/02/10-steps-to-creating-a-data-driven-culture

National Defense University Press. (n.d.). *A Strategic Leader's Guide to Transforming Culture in Large Organizations*. Retrieved from https://ndupress.ndu.edu/Media/News/Article/1219704/a-strategic-leaders-guide-to-transforming-culture-in-large-organizations/

Online HBS. (2023). *7 Ways to Improve Your Ethical Decision-Making. Business Insights Blog*. Retrieved from https://online.hbs.edu/blog/post/ethical-decision-making-process

USC Online Communication Degree. (n.d.). *Keys to Making Smart Business Decisions*. Retrieved from https://communicationmgmt.usc.edu/blog/the-5-keys-to-making-smart-business-decisions

Wharton Executive Education. (2016). *Make Better Decisions Under Uncertainty: Taking Charge of Chance. Wharton at Work*. Retrieved from https://executiveeducation.wharton.upenn.edu/thought-leadership/wharton-at-work/2016/02/better-decisions-under-uncertainty/

www.ingramcontent.com/pod-product-compliance
Lightning Source LLC
Chambersburg PA
CBHW070249230526
45470CB00002B/542